Clarence Stetson

Why Not Cycle Abroad Yourself?

What a bicylce trip in Europe costs, how to take it, how to enjoy it, with a narrative

of personal tours, illustrations and maps. Vol. 1

Clarence Stetson

Why Not Cycle Abroad Yourself?
What a bicylce trip in Europe costs, how to take it, how to enjoy it, with a narrative of personal tours, illustrations and maps. Vol. 1

ISBN/EAN: 9783337149437

Printed in Europe, USA, Canada, Australia, Japan

Cover: Foto ©Andreas Hilbeck / pixelio.de

More available books at **www.hansebooks.com**

Why Not Cycle Abroad Yourself?

WHAT A BICYCLE TRIP IN EUROPE COSTS, HOW TO TAKE IT, HOW TO ENJOY IT, WITH A NARRATIVE OF PERSONAL TOURS, ILLUSTRATIONS AND MAPS.

BY

CLARENCE STETSON.

COPYRIGHT 1898.

PUBLISHED BY F. & E. GREENEBAUM,
13 Spruce St., New York.

For Sale by The American News Company.
Paper, 50 Cents; Cloth, 75 Cents and $1.

CHAPTER I.

The Pleasures and Cheapness of a Bicycle Tour Abroad.

*And o'er the hills and far away
Beyond their utmost purple rim,
Beyond the night, across the day
Thro all the world she followed him.*
— TENNYSON

EARS ago Tennyson wrote these lines to describe the perigrinations of a young woman in love. The poet doesn't say how his hero and heroine traveled, so they may have taken the railroad train, or voyaged by an ocean steamer, or possibly they traveled by balloon, or had a bit of the magic carpet mentioned in the "Arabian Nights."

But if Tennyson were writing of to-day, we should have no hesitation in concluding how "she" followed him.

What would any sensible nineteenth century up-to-date young woman do nowadays if setting out on a journey beyond the night and across the day, to say nothing of going beyond the furthermost purple rim? Why, naturally she would get out her bicycle, read this little book which would tell her all she need to know, and start off throughout the world at an expense which would make her or anyone else think living in a Harlem flat dear by comparison, considering the returns achieved.

But seriously, even in this land of bicycles, where grown women would like to tuck their wheels under their pillows at night, just as they used to do with their dolls, in days gone by, are the possibilities of the bicycle fully understood? A change of scene is quite as necessary to health and contentment of mind as change of diet, and it is fair to believe that there are many American cyclists who would like to get away from the beaten track and cycle in Europe if they were not deterred by the lack of knowledge of how much it would cost and the way to do it, besides being overwhelmed at the prospect of wheeling in countries where they could not speak the language. Let me in a single round settle these two bugaboos of cycling abroad.

As to the expense: Aside from the first cost of the ocean passage a European tour on a bicycle costs no more than, if as much as, an ordinary summer outing at home under the same conditions and of a like duration. The truth is that the cheapness of a wheeling tour in Europe is really remarkable—if one wishes to make it cheap and knows how. As to languages one has no need of an interpreter. Abroad, as elsewhere, money talks and is the best interpreter you can possibly have. However, this statement is made with limitation. I have no wish to disparage the worth of linguistic attainments, and no one is further from belittling the value of a knowledge of French, for instance, with a smattering of as many other languages thrown in as you can conveniently get into your hand bag. Still, one can go as far as to say that with a fair idea, in advance, of what things ought to cost, and with all the information which it is our object to have comprised in this little volume, one can travel throughout Europe on a bicycle without being subjected either to extortion or petty annoyances, and with perfect ease, comfort and safety. I make this statement, too, not from any theoretical point of view. It is based on actual experience in Italy, where, ordinarily, nothing is spoken except the language of the country. There I have often stopped at a cafe to enquire the way to the next town in my choicest Italian, and have been understood to say that I wanted a bottle of their best Chianti. Still, such an experience is so novel, and you and your friends get so much amusement out of it, that it becomes a pleasant incident of the trip. Besides, it really isn't a serious matter if you get to your destination perhaps a bit later than you expected. You may be sure that the extra time will not have been without pleasure and profit.

In Holland, too, cyclists find that they might as well be deaf mutes as far as holding extended communication with the inhabitants goes. The fact is, that with good maps which can be obtained anywhere in Europe and which are made specially for the use cyclists, one doesn't need to do much talking, particularly if the route has been carefully studied beforehand. Still, one will find it very convenient to have in one's pocket one of Nutt's dictionaries, which are only about three or four inches long by two or three wide, and give you an astonishingly complete list of English words with the foreign equivalent in the language of whatever country you may find yourself in. These useful little volumes unite, too, the qualities of a dictionary and a conversational handbook, besides containing much general information in foot notes. With such able assistance and a map the most timid traveler will feel himself at home anywhere in Europe.

So much for any linguistic difficulties Now we'll get down to the solid facts of what is necessary to the successful accomplishment of a bicycle trip in Europe and the attendant expenses of the journey from the time you leave New York until the return trip is made.

Books, almost beyond number, have been written of ordinary trips to every corner of Europe, and Baedeker supplies every want of the ordinary tourist. Therefore, all information other than that of use to cyclists, and all incidents not of peculiar interest to them, will find no place in the following chapters.

Of course the bicycle, like the baby—I believe in families where expense is an item and they can't have both, they generally choose the former—is the first thing to be considered.

In the matter of the transportation of your wheel you have no reason for speculation as to the cost. All the steamship lines, no matter what may be the cost of a first cabin passage, have "pooled" their issues and have agreed upon a uniform rate of $2.50 for each wheel. It is required that your bicycle should be crated in some manner or other. In France, basket frames, which can be had for $5, are much in vogue, but a bicycle can readily be nailed up with light boards at a very moderate cost and in such a way as to answer every purpose; or any bicycle dealer will crate your wheel for you.

The initial expense of the ocean trip depends largely upon your tastes, inclinations and the place in Europe at which you wish to begin your actual wheeling. The rates on all steamships are about twenty per cent. higher between the last of April and the last of October than during the rest of the year. To give some basis of just named—from $85 to $107 as the lowest single first-class ticket through from New York to London; to Paris, $90 to $110; $75 to $100 to Southampton, Liverpool, Plymouth or Havre; $90 to $110 to Bremen or Hamburg. During the winter season these rates are reduced to the basis of about $80 to London. For outside staterooms, and those on the upper or promenade deck higher rates are charged. If you are willing to go second class, where often the accommodations are very good and the table excellent, you can travel at about 65 per cent. of these figures. Besides crossing on the great and best known lines there are other and extremely comfortable ways of getting across the Atlantic, if you are willing to spend a little more time at it. All the first class line steamers cross in about seven days. If you are willing to devote ten days to it you can go to London in the summer season, first class, on the Atlantic Transport or Leyland lines for $50 to $70. These steamers have "bilge keels"—an arrangement which practically prevents rolling—and while they carry cattle the cattle are all below decks, and out of sight, and are no source of annoyance. Many persons prefer these steamers because of their great steadiness. Their table has been highly commended.

Besides these steamers there are lines, not so well known as the first-class companies, which will carry you in very comfortable steamers to

Amsterdam for $75 to $80, or to Antwerp for $65 to $75. You can also go to Glasgow for from $50 to $80. All these prices are for single first-class tickets in the summer season. Winter rates are at a reduction, but under the new agreement between the steamship companies round trip tickets except on one or two lines are no longer offered at a discount. While winter rates are in force one can cross for as little as $45.

You will find it to your advantage, as soon as you have selected your European destination and the line by which you wish to reach it, to secure your staterooms at the earliest possible moment. The summer rush to Europe is now so heavy that all the rooms on some steamers are taken a month before the vessel sails.

If you decide to land at an English port—Southampton, Liverpool, or Plymouth, let us say—you will find wheeling thence to London an enjoyable experience. There are no customs duties in England on bicycles, and no irksome regulations governing the introduction of your wheel. The roads are admirable, the scenery, while quiet, is sweet and refreshing, and many of the towns on the way have interesting old churches or places of historical interest, the only drawback being that sometimes the rural inns leave much to be desired. If you land at Southampton you will find much to interest you at Winchester and Aldershot; your road from Plymouth brings you through Exeter,

THE WAY TO PARIS

Taunton, Bristol and Bath; from Liverpool you can make Manchester, the Peaks of Derby or Oxford, on your way to London. From London you can ride down to Dover through the lovely Kentish hills and Rochester and Canterbury, and take the boat at a small cost for Calais; or you can buy a railroad ticket by New Haven and Dieppe to Paris for $6, and ship your wheel as baggage; or you can get to the Continent in half a dozen other ways, for the most part agreeable and cheap.

Bicycling in England is so much like bicycling at home, among a people with a common language, and customs, which, though different, are really familiar to us, that no suggestions are needed for the assistance or comfort of the fortunate person who undertakes it. The only essential wherein it differs from bicycling in the United States is that the wheelman must keep to the left of the road instead of to the right.

If a tour in England is contemplated before going to the continent, I should certainly recommend the tourist to join the Touring Club of England, as that will entitle him to a card of membership, and by showing this he will avoid any question over duties on landing in France.

The imposition of duties on tourists' bicycles in France seems to depend upon certain conditions. I have known many Americans who on landing have had no difficulty whatsoever in persuading the French Custom House officials that they were merely tourists, and have been allowed thereupon to pass their bicycles free of duty. In other instances, however, the duty has been demanded, and no explanations would suffice to make the official change his mind on that point. Perhaps it makes a difference whether you see a French Custom House official before or after dinner. But after all, this isn't a very serious matter, and if the official insists upon your paying duty on your machine after you have explained to him that you are simply on a pleasure tour, the best thing to do is to pay the money and take a receipt. This receipt you present when you leave France, whether it is on your way back home or in crossing the frontier into some other country, and you receive your money back again. That is, if you take your bicycle outside of France within a year from the time you entered it. The duty anyway is only 25 cents a pound, which means that you are only tying up $5 or $6 during your stay in the country. The absurdity of taxing bicycles by the pound is easily seen when one stops to think that a most carefully made machine of extraordinary lightness. which may have cost $200, and may be the property of a millionaire, would pay less duty than the heavy old fashioned machine of some poor laboring man who could afford no better.

If you are going to France it is wise to become a member of the French Touring Club, because that enables you to take your bicycle in free of duty and gives you other substantial advantages, as will appear later. It is possible to join the Touring Club de France by applying to Mr. Francis S. Hesseltine, Delegue, Touring Club de France, 10 Tremont street, Boston, Mass. The following is the blank form which has to be filled out. The expense attached is only $1.20, which includes the admission fee and the annuaire which is issued by the Club monthly.

DEMANDE D'ADMISSION.

Je demande mon admission au TOURING-CLUB DE FRANCE.

Ci-joint: 5 francs, montant de la cotisation de l'annee courante, plus 1 fr. pour recevoir l'ANNUAIRE franco (*). (Le rachat de la cotisation est admis moyennant le versement d'une somme de Cent francs; il confere la qualite de Membre a vie).

Les candidats habitant les Colonies ou l'Etranger doivent joindre 1 franc pour le service de la Revue.

NOTA.—Le volume "Plans de Voyages' et d'Excursions" pour toute la France et pays voisins est joint a l'envoi moyennant un franc.

SIGNATURE:

Nom ....
Prenoms ....
Profession ....
    (Soit l'actuelle, soit l'ancienne.)
Nationalite ....
Decorations et distinctions honorifiques ....
    (*) Envoyer les mandats ou bons de poste au nom de M. P. Leroy, tresorier du T. C. F.

But such an application should be made at least six weeks or two months prior to the time fixed for your departure. If this course is pursued all trouble about entering your bicycle into France is done away with at once. There is another association in Boston which ladies traveling alone may find it to their interest to consult before taking the European trip. It is known as the "Women's Rest Tour Association." Its object is to furnish to women who travel for rest, study or pleasure, such practical advice and encouragement as shall enable them to travel independently, intelligently and economically. For membership in the Association and all particulars apply to No. 264 Boylston street, Boston, Mass.

CHAPTER II.

Information and General Advice.

IT HAS already been stated that there is no duty on entering your bicycle in England for touring purposes. For information as to joining the Cyclers' Touring Club apply to Mr. Frank W. Weston, United States Chief Consul, Boston. Mr. Weston will furnish information free, but applicants should send stamps for reply. The membership of this English cycling club is an international one, there being between forty and fifty thousand members already enrolled. Circulars of application for membership, information as to hand books, road maps, badges and all like details can be had on applying as above. The annual subscription fee is $1.35, while the entrance fee is thirty cents. The advantages of the club are detailed in their circulars and embody the following:

To encourage and facilitate touring in all parts of the world.

To provide riding or touring companions.

To protect its members against any infringement of the rights and privileges to which they are entitled, and to extend those rights and privileges wherever possible.

To secure special rates and increased privileges, and to appoint hotels and inns for the convenience of its members in all countries where cycling is practiced.

To appoint a consul in every town, who shall render to his fellow-members local information germane to the pastime unobtainable from other sources.

To similarly appoint official repairers, competent to remedy breakages and defects in machines.

To publish monthly an official gazette, to be supplied gratis to members only.

To compile and issue to members at reduced prices, maps and road books especially adapted to the requirements of the cyclist.

To inculcate and encourage an esprit de corps in the brotherhood of the wheel, and to uphold and promote the true interests of cycling the wide world over.

The L. A. W. is represented in England by the Foreign Marshal, Joseph Pennell, care J. S. Morgan & Co., 22 Old Broad Street, London, E. C.

FRANCE.

If you have made no other arrangements and have not joined the Touring Club de France, but have simply decided to pay duty on your wheel on landing in France, you will receive, on handing over the twenty-five cents per pound, a receipt for the sum, and the official will also attach a lead seal to your wheel. This is what is known as having your bicycle plombe. The seal is removed when you claim your deposit at any frontier point by which you may leave France. French citizens pay $2 a year as a tax on their machine. The imposition of this tax on bicycles brings in something like $150,000 in Paris alone, which is about one-fifth of the sum received from the tax throughout the whole of France. In road riding you will notice that the hills are nearly always marked with posts, which warn the rider of their dangers either in the way of steepness or sharp turns. But in France even ladies can easily ride many of the hills marked as dangerous. The edict of the Prefet of Police in Paris says that your machine must bear a bell or gong which can be heard at least fifty yards, and in Paris particularly one must be very certain to have some sort of a light as darkness approaches. Chinese lanterns carried in the hand are in very general use. In streets crowded with pedestrians the rider must dismount and push his wheel. Cyclists are not allowed to form in groups so as to obstruct the public ways or cross funerals or military processions. They are forbidden to cycle on footpaths reserved for pedestrians except in special instances where the road is impassable, and then they are expected to moderate their speed.

The French Minister of Public Works has compelled by decree all railroads to carry cycles as baggage and makes them responsible for any damage. The rules of the road for keeping to the right and other details are the same as in the United States. All citizens of

France who ride bicycles are required to have their names and addresses on their machines, and it is just as well for even a casual visitor to take the same precaution, although he may not be liable to the same regulations, being a non-resident. In fact, I have ridden a bicycle two years in Paris without ever having been asked to show my plaque, or official certificate. Still, if you are not living at a hotel, observation of this provision of the law will probably be demanded.

The advantages to the members of the Touring Club de France are quite pronounced. One of the chief is the freedom with which you can cross the frontiers of the neighboring countries without being troubled by custom officials for a deposit on your machine, for the club has obtained this concession in behalf of its members from most of the adjacent nations. Incidentally, many hotels give a discount, in most cases of ten per cent., and, moreover, one is assured of courteous treatment and special consideration if one displays a badge or card of membership in this club, which now numbers more than sixty thousand members. The club also has a representative in every town and city in France always willing to give you any advice and information possible. The club's headquarters are situated in the Rue Coq-Heron, No. 5, Paris. It is well always to have photograph on your card of identity, a fac simile of which is appended.

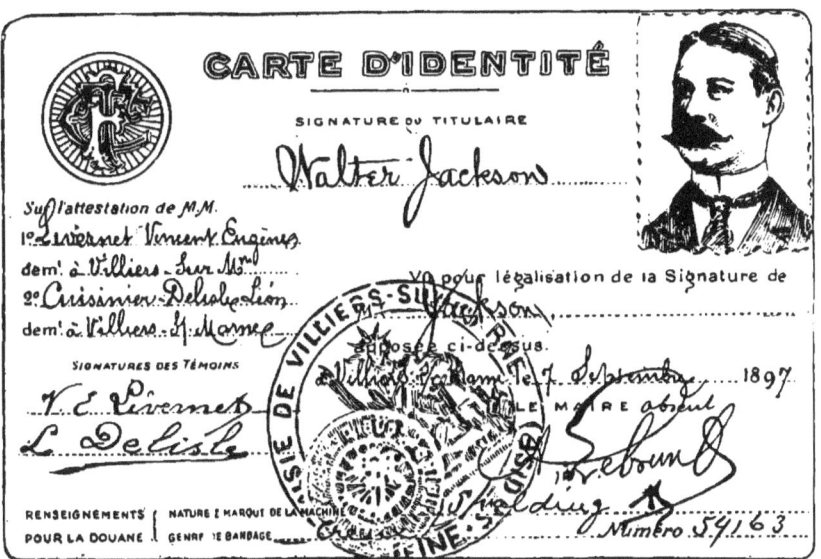

BELGIUM.

Before making a trip to Belgium, it is well to get a special permit from the headquarters of the club in the Rue Coq-Heron, as the Belgium authorities are more particular in such matters than those that one finds on almost any other frontier.

Tourists not members of the Touring Club de France have to make a deposit at the Belgium Custom House of a sum amounting to twelve per cent. ad valorem. This amount is refunded when you take your machine out of the country. The exemption allowed to the Touring Club members is for six months only. There is always less trouble getting your wheel across the frontier if you are riding it and not traveling by train. Persons who are going to travel in Europe by rail are advised not to take their wheels with them at all unless they are going to make a long stay at some given point. You can hire very fair bicycles anywhere in Europe.

GERMANY.

The duty on bicycles in Germany amounts to three cents a pound, if the machine is for sale. The tourists pay nothing—no deposit is required. The foreign consul of the League of American Wheelmen in Germany can always be consulted for advice and information. His address is Friedrich Schleicher, Duren Rheinland, Bonnerstrasse, 16, Germany.

AUSTRIA.

In Austria, by special decree, you are compelled to swear that your wheel is not for sale and that you are simply a temporary visitor in Austria; you then deposit $10 at the Custom House, but this deposit is refunded when you take your wheel out of the country.

ITALY.

Here you deposit a sum amounting to a little more than $8 as a guarantee that your wheel is not for sale. Members of the Touring Club de France are exempt on presenting their card of membership, but you must not forget to declare your wheel, in crossing the frontier again, on your way out of Italy; otherwise your club will be called upon to pay the duty on your machine. If you have made a deposit it is given back to you when you leave the country.

SWITZERLAND.

The duty here amounts to six cents a pound, and the conditions are the same as in Italy, members of the Touring Club de France being exempt. On each frontier a lead seal will be attached to your machine and will be removed when you cross it again.

DENMARK.

Here you deposit with the Custom House ten per cent. ad valorem with a guarantee you will not sell your wheel. The deposit will only be refunded at the Custom House where the entry was made, unless by special permit.

EGYPT.

Duty, eight per cent. ad-valorem, of which only seven per cent. will be refunded. Be particular to get the proper receipt for your money deposited.

GREECE.

Cyclists have to pay first an octroi duty of forty cents payable at point of entry. This will be returned. There is still another duty of $2, which will be returned to you less $1 for expenses, or with a slightly additional charge if you do not leave the country at the same Custom House.

LUXEMBOURG.

Duty here is about three cents a pound, the members of the Touring Club de France being exempt.

NETHERLANDS.

Duty is five per cent. ad valorem, but tourists enter without having to make a deposit or pay any duty.

PORTUGAL.

Tourists pay a duty of twenty-seven per cent. ad valorem, but can get their money back on leaving the country by any point where there is a custom house.

SPAIN.

Here the duty amounts to about six cents a pound, on depositing which you receive a pass good for six months, for which you pay the sum of twenty cents. In this country there are many petty formalities connected with getting your pass, and if the slightest mistake is made in your declaration, or you in any way misunderstand the requirements, you do not get your money back when you leave the country. Therefore it is better here to engage somebody beforehand to arrange the matter for you.

SWEDEN.

Here a deposit of fifteen per cent. ad valorem is demanded, and in order to have the money refunded you must leave the country by the port of entry. If you remain in the country more than sixty days your deposit is forfeited.

TURKEY.

Duty required amounts to eight per cent. ad valorem, of which only seven per cent. is returned to you and you are lucky if you get that.

RUSSIA.

The payment of $7.80 on each machine is here required. You can't get this money back unless you go out by the port of entry, except by obtaining a special permit.

ROUMANIA.

Here you pay $1.55 on each machine, which will be returned to you at the port of entry or elsewhere by special permit.

Of course I needn't warn any cyclist to be sure and start with his wheel in perfect order. It is also well to take duplicate pieces of all parts of the machine which are liable to break or get out of order. The chain, the nuts and the other parts which you may require for your special machine may not be obtainable in every small town in Europe. Of course some cyclists are born mechanics and can fix their own wheels; such are to be congratulated, as the others may have to put up with bungling work in the way of repairs. But no one will make any mistake in taking as many duplicate parts of his machine along as possible. It is well to remember, too, when you are boxing your machine for the Atlantic trip, to cover all the nickel parts with a little vaseline or whatever may be your favorite preparation for preventing rust. And don't forget to take along a good stick of graphite for the chain.

Wheeling in the more remote country districts is much more attractive and picturesque than going over the same ground by railroad, and, in fact, some of the most delightful trips are those furthest from where the railroad runs. Odd little hotels with quaint surroundings are to be found everywhere, and cheapness of rates and an honest display of hospitality seem to go hand in hand. Besides, and more particularly is it the case if there are ladies in the party, you will find yourself objects of extraordinary interest wherever you go. Of course the saving in railroad fares lightens very much the cost of the trip and bicyclists always get the best of rates at the hotels.

The only uncertainty as to the pleasure of touring on a wheel in Europe, is, of course, due to the weather. But naturally, when it rains, you don't wheel. In such a case if merely caught in a light shower, the gauze rubber cape, weighing only a few ounces, which you should include in the effects which you carry on your machine, would be sufficient to protect you until you arrive at the nearest town or village where there is a railway or a tramway. From there you can make for the largest town or city by rail, and there is sure to be one not many miles away. Once there, the novelty of finding yourself amid new surroundings lessens very much the weariness of waiting for the rain to stop. I remember when it rained for three days, near Verona, while I was riding with a party through Italy, but in spite of the rain that mouldy old city furnished such an array of attractions that we wouldn't have much cared if another flood had come along. Moreover, nearly everywhere in Europe the roads are so constructed that they dry very quickly, and one can proceed on one's way almost immediately after the rain has stopped.

When you do take a train with your bicycle it is well always to remember the porter liberally, bearing in mind that liberality means from six to ten cents, and he will handle your wheel more carefully than he otherwise would. And, in case you have time, it is well to supervise the operation of putting it in the baggage car yourself. There are no "checks" for baggage in Europe, but you can register it at a small expense and the register amounts to much the same thing.

I presume that I needn't tell anyone that it would be the height of folly to attempt a European tour without a brake; they are useful, particularly in cities like Paris, where one finds the most careless drivers in the world, to aid you in stopping quickly on the crowded boulevards as well as on many of the hills in the neighborhood of Paris, to say nothing of being absolutely necessary when touring in Switzerland. Taking a coast down a mountain of say some forty miles with nothing but your shoe for a brake would doubtless prove very bad for the shoe—but probably if you made such an attempt with no other precaution provided you would find yourself where you wouldn't have any need for shoes or bicycles either. Some cyclists say that they have been greatly aided in descending steep and long declivities by attaching a fir tree to their saddle by means of a rope eight or ten feet long. I never saw this tried, but I have seen two delicate women ride down the Grimsel and the Simplon Passes with no other aid in holding back their machines than that which they were able to get from back pedalling and the judicious use of the brake. One source of much trouble to cyclists in Europe, particularly in the rural districts are the hob nails which drop out of the peasants' shoes. These nails always insist on standing on their heads, and being sharp and oftentimes two inches long, they have no difficulty in giving a pneumatic tire nervous prostration.

To lessen the chances of picking up tacks or even bits of glass, some French riders use a very simple little device. They attach a little wire across the fork where the wheel turns about a sixteenth of an inch from the tire. Their argument is that the tack does not puncture the rubber when the wheel first touches it, but merely picks it up so that on the first half revolution of the wheel after it has touched a tack or bit of glass, the object comes against this wire and is knocked off the tire before it touches the ground again. Those who have tried this device say they have never had a puncture since they fastened the wire just above both wheels. It certainly will cost no wheelman anything to try it.

CHAPTER III.

From Havre to Paris.

LET us now suppose that you have arrived at Havre or some other point on that part of the French coast, and have gotten by the custom house officials, either with your French Touring card, or that of the English organization, or, lacking either of these, have paid duty, or have persuaded the inspector that you are a bona fide tourist, with the result that you are not obliged to make the usual deposit.

Once off the steamer, the first impulse of the eager cyclist is to mount his wheel, and having seen that his cyclometer is in order, set off for Paris. I should, however, hardly advise all tourists, unless limited to a very brief stay in France, to do this. At the moment, you very likely find yourself unprovided with the proper maps, and immediately after the voyage you are not in a condition to get the full enjoyment out of the bicycle or anything else. On the other hand, Paris is only five hours away by rail and the ticket costs less than $5. Still, if you want to ride through one of the prettiest parts of the country, and can let Paris wait, there is nothing to prevent your setting out on your journey at once. It is an easy matter to ship your baggage by train to the Gare St. Lazare at Paris, where you will find it awaiting your arrival in the Consigne, and there you will have to open it for the Octroi or City Customs officials. Baggage in Europe doesn't go free as it does in this country, even if you accompany it yourself. Sixty pounds is the limit one is allowed in Europe on a single ticket, and where one sends baggage ahead, there is no reasonable system of transportation similar to our express companies in America. For instance, one can send a trunk from Boston to New York for forty-five cents. But for the same distance in Europe you would pay six or seven cents a pound on the grande vitesse or express train. If you send the baggage by the petite vitesse, or freight train, from almost any given point in Europe to another, it costs about half as much as by the express, but you must count on a wait anywhere from a week to ten days for a distance say of three hundred miles.

The writer recalls, in his own case, that on leaving Milan, Italy, for Nice by the way of Genoa and Ventimiglia he sent his trunks, weighing sixty pounds, to Nice with the stipulation that they should be put on the express train only. The charge amounted to more than

$5 and riding to Nice on his bicycle he got there two days ahead of his trunks. Therefore it is apparent that one wants to get along with as little baggage as possible. In fact, the ordinary mistake that one makes in setting out on such a trip is to take too much. It is astonishing how much one can take on the bicycle, and the expense of sending on your baggage is greatly lessened if you carry enough on your wheel so as to be obliged to connect with your trunks only about once in ten days. All the necessities of the toilet, reading and writing materials, changes of underclothing and a rubber cape can be carried on the frame of your bicycle without materially increasing the difficulty of its propulsion, if the weight is carefully distributed.

Personally, I have never had the patience, after arriving on French soil, to submit to the delay of getting to the most seductive city on earth except by the most rapid means of locomotion which presented itself. I have made tours in Normandy and Brittany, but have always taken Paris as the basis of operations.

However, for the benefit of those who, after landing, decide to go to Paris on their wheels, I append the following bits of a description of such a trip from the pen of Arthur K. Peck, who took it himself in the summer of 1897, and embodied his impressions in one of a series of letters to the Boston Sunday Herald. Mr. Peck says:

My journey awheel commenced at the Port of Havre, France, and my first day's journey was inward througn a pleasing section of Normandy. Packed in the little case in the frame of my machine, and strapped on the carrier of the handle bar was all my luggage, which included a rubber suit for protection from the rain, various duplicate parts of a wheel for use in case of a breakage, and a repair kit and tools for tire mending in case of puncture. Across my back I slung a small camera, with the expectation of bringing back to America with me wayside photographs, stray shots of picturesque little nooks, odd scenes, the people, their homes—views which are not to be purchased.

Before starting, I made a most minute inspection of all parts of my bicycle, trying every bolt and adjustment, for, while it is true that the prominent American manufacturers have agents in foreign cities, and they are supposed to be well supplied with duplicate parts, not infrequently they are "just out of that particular part." It behooves one, therefore, to exercise a close guardianship over one's bicycle from the moment of arrival in Europe.

Havre, according to the guide book, has little to interest the traveler, and so, after a short ramble about the city, I wheeled along toward Graville, a small suburb of Havre, and one of the chain of towns through which I must pass en route to Rouen.

Continuing my journey, I soon found myself

on a fine stretch of road, which brought me into the agricultural district, with its green pastures and verdant hills. Here whole fields of grain were dotted with bright flowers of variegated hues. The abundance of wild flowers to be seen at certain stages of the journey added much to the picturesqueness of the scenes. I passed through the dead little seaport town of Honfleur, distinguished from the fact that about six centuries ago Henry V. of England took it and later some of his successors returned it. Havre has long since taken away its trade as a seaport.

Ten miles out I made my first inquiry, asking three natives of St. Romain the way to the next town, La Remuee. Not one of them seemed to know. My persistency was rewarded, however, when I asked the route to Lillebonne, which one of them seemed to know, though it was twelve miles away.

There was a most exhilarating coast of a mile or more down into this town. On one of the surrounding heights could be seen looming up above the trees the gray tower of the ruined castle where William the Conqueror, one thousand years ago, extended a cordial invitation to the nobles to visit old England and increase their real estate holdings, which invitation we are advised on good authority was accepted.

As I entered the town from one side a regiment of infantry marched in from the other. In advance came a French officer scorching in on a bicycle. All about the place on the ground were little heaps of refreshments of bread, rare meat, etc., contributions for the tired men of the invading host. I did want to take a picture of the scene, but with a discretion born of previous experience, and acting under advice written in my little book of "don'ts," saying, "don't take pictures of anything military and thus avoid unpleasant consequences," I hunted up a place to have my noon lunch and had what a Frenchman calls his breakfast.

Continuing on my journey, I tried for a few days the experience of travelling without maps, but found it unsatisfactory, and the guide post system of Brittany not so excellent as that of Normandy. I found Brittany quite hilly as a whole, more so than Normandy. At times on the journey toward Paris I would come to a long level plain and would ride for miles on a straight, level road, as was the case when entering Chartres. In one case only did I lose my course, and that was due to accepting the advice of a peasant seated at a cross road. I believe I was directed to Noce instead of Nogent. I succeeded, however, after going four miles out of the way, in finding the main highway and righted myself. I was in no amiable frame of mind at the mishap, particularly as the roads were hilly and the weather was hot.

At Chartres there was a magnificent cathedral to see, and then, by a long day's journey, I counted on reaching Paris. Eighty miles from the capital I saw the first guide post bearing the word Paris, and from there on I found myself watching the kilometre posts, and unconsciously translating into miles each distance marked. I passed through the town of Maintenon, and dismounted to view the old chateau of Madame de Maintenon. Not far distant I reached a little town, which in appearance seemed to me to approach the nearest to a deserted village I had ever seen in all my wanderings. As I jogged along over the rough stone pavements through the main and only street of the town, looking right and left for some signs of life, I wondered whether this dead town was the Chelsea or Pompeii of France. There were no children playing in the street, every door was closed, and shutters were up at all the windows. Even a store, which had over the door the word "Novelties," seemed to have given up its business, for the shutters there, too, were up.

During the first few days of my journey in Normandy my ideas of the topography of the country underwent quite a change. I had expected to see a country not unlike Cape Ann and the North shore, and to encounter a succession of steep hills. Instead, I found about two steep hills a day, and long, level stretches between. The fact that my first day in France, heavily laden as the bicycle was with my baggage, I had covered sixty-two miles, from Havre to Rouen; had seen the points of interest and made a side trip to the ruins of an old abbey of the seventh century at Jumieges, shows quite clearly the topographical conditions. As for the roads, no adjective is good enough to describe their excellence. It is no exaggeration to compare them to our park roads in quality, though not of course, possessing the great breadth.

Though following the Seine, generally speaking, I caught only an occasional glimpse of the river, once at the quaint old town of Caudebec, again at Jumieges, where the banks of the river suggest portions of the Hudson, and at Duclaire.

The clocks were striking six when I caught my first glimpse of Rouen in the valley below. "Dangerous hill, look out," said the signboard of the Tourist Club de France, and so with brake well in hand, down the hill I coasted and dashed into the streets of the city of Rouen.

I passed through Rambouillet, and saw the park and forest. It was here Francis I. died at his chateau. As I was proceeding on my way I met a young man on his wheel riding in the opposite direction to which I was going. He turned about and we rode to Paris together. He knew some English, and when he could not find the exact word necessary he invariably fell back on the expression "all right." We passed over an extremely hilly district, going to Versailles, but the surroundings were beautiful. I left the palace and the gardens of Versailles as a part of my Paris programme, and proceeded without delay over the main road to St. Cloud, and from there through the Bois de Boulogne to Paris.

It is of course an essential feature, and in fact a necessity, in touring that the cycler be well equipped with the best of maps. The geographical knowledge of the peasant is quite elementary, and generally speaking, the most distant point with which he has any acquaintance is the adjoining village. Under such circumstances, unless the tourist has familiarized himself with the names of intervening towns, all his queries will be to the villagers as complex conundrums.

The foreign maps are works of art and encyclopedias of information. Aside from the maps for military purposes, there are special maps for cycling equally as elaborate, showing the great highways, and distinguishing them from the ordinary routes, giving the distances in kilometres, between towns, and in the mountainous regions the elevations and distinctive signs mark the location of places of interest—chateaux, ruins, convents, glaciers, beautiful points of view, etc.

Supplementary to the accessories of travel above mentioned, the standard guide books enable one to get a very comprehensive knowledge of the interesting places to be seen in every town and of the towns themselves.

In reviewing the trip, I can speak only in the

highest terms of the treatment received at the places where I stopped. Everywhere I received the most courteous acquiescence to my requests to be directed on my journey. I found the food excellent and the roads perfection. The scenery at times was charming, at times beautiful and picturesque. I had slept in country inns, and listened to the church bell chimes of Normandy ringing out the quarter hour, or perhaps the curfew note—bells whose very tone told of old age, and churches whose moss-covered, gray walls had been standing for centuries. I had wandered through ruined abbeys, castles and palaces. I entered towns bristling with fortifications, the scenes of wars and siege and battle with English monarchs. I saw the home and final resting place of the Norman ruler who made whole chapters of early English history a record of his triumphs.

Such are the pleasant experiences Mr. Peck records of the ride from Havre to Paris.

CHAPTER IV.

"In Gay Paree."

WHETHER it was done by rail, or whether you rode in on your wheel, I am going to take it for granted that you made the journey from where you left your steamer and arrived in Paris with all the cyclist's capacity of enjoyment of the material things of this life. Whether you send your baggage ahead, or whether it comes on the train with you, you will experience very little trouble with the Octroi authorities at the Gare St. Lazare. The chances are they will make only a very cursory examination, but it is well to be careful not to have any matches, tobacco or wine with you.

Of course, on arriving in the city for which Napoleon the Little did so much in spite of the ill he wrought for the rest of France, the question of where to go is the most important one that confronts you. On this subject I can only say that Paris, perhaps more than any other place in the world, can furnish hotels of any kind suited to the purse of any one. It is at once the dearest and cheapest city of modern times. If you have no friends in Paris and have made, no previous arrangement, any hotel will do for the first twenty-four hours. The largest and best known for such a transient stay are the Grand, the Terminus and the Continental. They all have the advantage of being easily pronounced, too. I know an American who prefers the Hotel de France et Choiseul to any hotel in Paris, but he can't stay there, because he can't pronounce the name when he wants to take a cab. The Chatham in the Rue d' Aunou and the St. Petersburg in the Rue Caumartin are also central, and in fact there are myriads of hotels that one can go to for a short stay while getting settled. In any of these hotels two persons can have a good room from $2 to $2.50 a day which includes electric lights and service, and you are free to take your meals where you like. You will find excellent English and American cooking and English spoken at 'Fred's" in the Rue Caumartin, near the corner of the Rue Auber, and at Pulaski's at No. 404 Rue St. Honore. Pulaski also imports American oysters. As for table d'hote at prices ranging from thirty, fifty and sixty cents up to a dollar, their name is legion. I insert the menu of one of them in order to give you an idea of what these places furnish, though I believe the particular restaurant mentioned here exists no longer.

Restaurant Table-d'Hôte LECLERCQ

37 Chaussée-d'Antin (à l'Entresol)

ORDINAIRE EST REPRIS POUR 40 c EN ECHANGE D'AUTRE VIN

Les Plats au Gratin se commandent d'avance

Petit Mâcon 80 c. Bᵗᵉ remplaçant 1/2 Bᵗᵉ 30 c de Supplément

Menu du 13 Janvier 1897

Potages
Soupe au fromage
Potiron

Hors-d'Œuvre
Céleris en rave
Anchois

Entrées
Cassoulet toulousaine
~~Filet~~
Côte de porc s' tomate
Poulet rôti froid
Rumsteck Jardinière
Gigot Rôti froid ~~~~

Poissons & Légumes
Merlans frits & Vinbl.
~~~~
Côte de veau à l'oseille
Choux bruxelles sautés
Flageolets Mᵉ d'hôtel
Macédoine de légumes
Salsifis sautés

Fromages
Brie — Suisse — Camembert

Desserts
Compote de poires — Pommes cuites
Pruneaux — Pommes — Oranges
Mandarines — Gaufrettes Biscuits
Galettes Dumoir — Fruits à l'eau de vie

These places are all well lighted and served by waiters in evening dress. The largest one at present where a menu of astonishing variety is given, is in the Place de la Trinite at the corner of la Rue Blanche. Here the dinner with wine is only thirty cents if you are looking for that sort of thing. The Place de la Trinite is directly back of the Opera, and is reached by passing through the Rue de la Chaussee d'Antin. For breakfast one of the Duval establishments will be found very satisfactory, as the menu is varied and the prices are cheap, though the portions are small. Anyone will direct you to the Duval establishment nearest to the place where you happen to be staying. I give here a Duval menu which will give you an idea of the variety and the prices, and it may also prove both amusing and profitable for the reader who is not over conversant with the French to get out his dictionary and see if he can puzzle out a breakfast order.

In summer the table d'hotes in the Champs Elysees, along the Avenue de la Grande Armee and at the Touring Club and the Chalet du Cycle in the Bois du Boulogne are always attractive, being enlivened by music and rendered dazzling by myriads of multi-colored lights.

However, if economy is the order of the day, the morning after your arrival you will do well to invest three cents in a copy of the European edition of the New York Herald, in the columns of which you will find plenty of advertisers who

take boarders at from five to seven francs a day, and even less by the month. That is to say, $1.40 a day will cover all your living expenses. If you are going to make a protracted stay in Paris, suitable rooms can be had on either side of the Seine for from forty francs, or $8 a month up. You will have little trouble in Paris in keeping your bicycle near you, and when you are on the street, the nearer you keep it to you the better. Most of the hotels have some arrangement for bicycles, and if you are in a private family or have rooms high up anywhere you will never find any difficulty in locating a man in the vicinity who makes a business of taking care of your wheel for six cents a day or $2 a month. When I lived in a hotel where there was no place downstairs for keeping a wheel, I found the valet de chambre only too willing to take my wheel up to my room. For taking two wheels up and bringing them down again he was amply repaid with ten cents, which made it a good deal cheaper than leaving a wheel en garage, as the French call it, outside. The advantage of this system is that you only pay for your wheel days when you use it instead of every day when you leave it en garage, and you also have it where you can look after it yourself if you care to.

In riding in Paris you must be careful to light your lamps or carry a Chinese lantern in your hand as darkness comes on; also have a clear-voiced bell, which the police edict says must be loud enough to be heard at least fifty yards.

If you get caught after dark without a lamp you can get a Chinese lantern at either a grocery store or a cigar store. A cigar store is indicated by a red light, and it is here also that you have to buy your stamps. If you can't find a cigar store or Bureau de Tabac, just ask anybody for the nearest epicerie. Don't be alarmed, it is only a grocery store. The lanterns are called lampions, and the price, together with the candle, varies from four to six cents, and depends generally on the dimensions of your accent.

If you are going to make a business of riding while you are in Paris, it is well to live in the Champs Elysees quarter, or on the Avenue de la Grande Armee itself; but if ycu do live downtown, in going to the Bois you will find it better to go up the Boulevard Haussmann or up the Champs Elysees. There is a car track, but less traffic on the Boulevard Haussmann and the wooden pavement furnishes excellent wheeling. But if you do decide to go up the Champs Elysees, don't follow the Boulevard de Capucines to the Rue Royale, but turn off to your left at the Rue Cambon, which has an asphalted pavement, and where there are very few carriages.

The Rue Cambon will take you to the Rue de Rivoli, where it is only a step to the Place de la Concorde, and then there is a straight-away ride up to the Arc de Triomphe. The other side of the Place de l'Arc de Triomphe, the Avenue la

Grande Armee begins with its special path reserved for cyclists. At the foot of this path is the well-known Cafe des Sports. In stopping at these cafes, never leave your wheel against the curb or any neighboring tree. This is against the police regulations, and is also dangerous, as you are apt to lose your wheel if you take your eyes off of it for a moment. But at all cafes, nowadays, accommodations are furnished for cyclists; but never give your wheel up to the commissaire without getting a ticket. An Englishman gave his wheel to the commissaire of the Criterion Cafe, in front of the Hotel Terminus, while he went in for dinner, and when he came out the wheel was gone. The proprietor refused to be responsible on the ground that the gentleman had not taken a ticket from his employe. In most of the cafes in the Bois, and nearly everywhere you ride, you will find Postes de Secours, where the injured can be looked after without delay. At many cafes are workmen with kits of tools sufficiently complete to mend anything except the ways of their patrons. Nearly all these cafes have orchestras, and one can pass an hour or even more most entertainingly in watching the ever-changing stream of cycling humanity as it ebbs in and out with everything new and odd in the way of costumes that one can imagine, and some that one never would have imagined.

In Paris, a Frenchman always regards any woman who rides a bicycle in a skirt either as

"HOW ARE YOU, YANKEE?"

an American or as an English girl, and she is apt to be greeted, as she flits by, with such expressions as "Oh, yes," "I speak English," "You are a jolie mees," and if he can't go as far as that, he is quite certain to greet you with "All right." It is a fact, however, that some French women prefer a skirt to the oftentimes hideous bloomers. Once, when I was coming back with a party through the Bois, one of the riders, who happened to be a most demure young French woman, was accosted by an impossible young French person of the chemical blonde type with "How are you, Yankee?" The lady addressed was unable to resist making a few comments in her native tongue, and she of the culotte was so astonished to find out that she of the skirt was a compatriot that she promptly fell off her wheel—much to the amusement of the crowd who had been watching her antics.

CHAPTER V.

Encore "Paree."

ASIDE from the idiot who will call out to you, "Yes, mees," and "All right," just because he wants to air his English, there is another pest who occasionally annoys ladies riding alone, no matter how carefully they have tried to choose an hour for their outing, when the Bois ought to be tolerably unfrequented. Still, this individual is more obnoxious than dangerous. The French "masher" will ogle and will sometimes say a few things that will make an English or an American girl wish she were a man for a few moments, but that's as far as he will go. From what I have seen of the type, I think he is more to be despised than feared, and should say that any self-respecting woman can ride in Paris without being subjected to a greater chance of annoyance than she would be at home.

Naturally, she will ignore any remarks addressed to her directly and affect the role of a deaf mute when things are said not directly at her, but meant for her all the same. Then again, she should not be disturbed at any "oddities" of costume. There is a censor who supervises such things in Paris and the police carry out his orders carefully. She may see things that will be so out of joint with her ideas of the beautiful as to cause an involuntary gasp and an exclamation, "Oh, how horrid!" "How can she!" but nothing more. For instance, "la culotte" (bloomers or tights would be our English word for it, depending on the cut of the particular culotte in question) isn't really shocking. Any old ballet girl in America presents herself in public in a costume which wouldn't be permitted even to a Parisian cyclist, without keeping an American girl away from the theatre. Still, you will see things of strange and uncanny character. For instance, some of the French young women who cycle have conceived the idea that it is the proper thing to wear socks. I say socks advisedly, for that is exactly what they are. They are cut like those of the male biped, only more on the Harlem flat plan; that is to say, they are smaller. They come up a little above the tops of the high laced shoe worn by the French rider and leave the rest of her leg bare to the knee. All classes of society in France wear the culotte, but those who ride the bicycle bare legged, it is fair to say, are not received at the Elysee.

Of these young women, let it be said to their credit—and it's very difficult for them to get

MEMBERS OF THE BARE-LEGGED CONTINGENT.

credit—that they never say anything which their foreign or more proper sisters cannot hear, nor do they insult them by word or look. Of course, the visitor may hear things that may be a little outre, but one will have to live so long in Paris to understand their "argot" or slang that one would be so old that it wouldn't make much difference what anybody said.

Besides the individual of the "masher" type, there used to be another character who did business in the Bois. The last I knew the police were looking out for him and he may exist no more, but this is the adventure that one American girl had with him: She had taken an early morning ride through the Bois and was returning through a path reserved for cyclists when a respectable looking man bowed to her politely and apologetically informed her that her tire was deflated. She looked down at her hind tire and saw that it was. The man, who was in cycling costume, politely offered to blow it up for her. Of course she very naturally suspected nothing, and when the man had finished pumping in the air he put on the cap, and rising to his feet, said: "I think that'll do, I'll just see." Whereupon he jumped lightly into the saddle and rode off, and it may be added that he hasn't got back yet.

The wheel was a new Columbia which the young woman had just got from home, and as she was quite as tall as the man it suited him perfectly. It was afterwards explained to her that this man makes a business of this particular thing. He waits patiently till he sees a woman or a young person with a tire that needs blowing up, and then addresses them as he did in this case. What the American girl said at the moment doesn't appear, but she was obliged to take a carriage home after reporting her case to the nearest Poste de Police. She did say afterwards that what made her maddest about it all was the provoking way in which the man looked back at her over his shoulder and called out with a winning smile, "Oui, c'est bien gonfle." "He had no need to tell me that it was well blown up," she said, "I could see that for myself."

At the restaurant of the Touring Club, or Grossetetes, at the entrance of the Bois as one enters it from the foot of the Avenue de la Grande Armee, one always finds a crowd from noon until midnight during the cycling season. There is also the music of an orchestra as well as that of women's voices and popping corks. An excellent table d'hote dinner is served here with wine and coffee for four francs or eighty cents.

Not much further along, on the way to the Gate of Suresne, you will notice on your left the sign d'Harmenonville; here you will see the swell women of the half world, the Emilie d'Alencons and Liane de Pougys of Paris. Of course, at home the cyclists would not even admit the existence of such persons, but in Paris, where they are included by all the newspapers in "those present" at the first nights of all the theatres, alongside of the names of society women, it is just as well to admit that they are very much in evidence in this gay capital.

"OUI C'EST BIEN GONFLE."

Then on to the Chalet du Cycle, past the club grounds where young Parisians of sporting taste play tennis and polo, to the Gate at Suresne, where the chalet will be found just to the left. If one goes through the gate and across the bridge one finds oneself on the most direct route to St. Germain and Versailles. But let us stop at the chalet. There one can see more queer scenes illustrative of the Parisian bicycle world in an hour than in any other one given spot.

As elsewhere, the orchestra plays incessantly, only pausing long enough for one of its members to pass the hat from time to time. There is no table d'hote at this resort, but an excellent dinner a la carte is served in little tents in the garden or in the casino itself, if one prefers. This is perhaps the most popular resort for bicyclists in the neighborhood of Pairs, and on the last Grand Prix Day the man in charge of the garage told me that he gave out checks for 12,000 bicycles checked there by patrons who had stopped to get a drink and look at one another.

This seems an enormous number of bicycles for one cafe to look after in one day, but when you consider that there was a rushing business from early morning till midnight and bicycles are even hung up in the trees to get them out of the way, it may be that the number left there was not exaggerated. One thing that will strike the Americans here, as in other resorts, will be the large number of automobiles of all sorts and descriptions which will come through the gates without causing the bicyclists any trepidation. In fact, so many of these are used in Paris that in places like the Chalet du Cycle there is a place set apart for them. If possible, get a seat immediately in front of the gate, where you will have a good chance to size up the eccentric costumes which are sure to present themselves in a never changing array; some are attractive and some are not; some risque to a degree, while others, by their very demureness, serve the wearer's purpose best; in fact, one sees exactly what one might expect to see in a country where the bride and groom sometimes go to the church for the wedding ceremony on a tandem, the groom in evening dress and the bride in the conventional gown of white satin, though cut a trifle shorter than usual and all the wedding party also mounted on wheels.

It is well to realize, too, that if you find yourselves interested observers of the French, they are equally critical of the foreigners, and for that reason it is always as well to make oneself as little conspicuous as possible. I remember noticing one day a party of Americans who were evidently in charge of a young woman who felt her responsibilities very much because she spoke a little French. She caused all the French people present a great deal of amusement, and her compatriots, who happened to notice the incident, a great deal of embarrassment, by the way in which she insisted, in very bad French, that the waiter should take away two syphons of seltzer, declaring that he was trying to cheat her, as the one that they had already was quite enough. As no charge is made for seltzer at such cafes, and a sign, "Eau de Seltz, gratuite," was displayed prominently on most all the trees, the assertiveness of the young woman was all the more ridiculous. It was simply another one of these cases where a little knowledge is a dangerous thing.

After you have become familiar with the Bois and are looking for change of scene, perhaps it will occur to you to ride over to the Latin Quarter for a brief visit to the Cafe d'Harcourt and other similar cafes made famous by the student patronage which they all depend on so largely. Of course, if you want to witness this scene in full action, you want to go in the evening. It is only necessary to cross the Seine by the bridge at the Place de la Concorde and ride up the Boulevard St. Germain to the "Boule-Miche," as the Boulevard St. Michel is commonly called. There you will see revelry by night and know that you are in the Latin Quarter without asking any one.

Opinions of Paris vary. I cite one here from the pen of a fair contributor to the Ladies' Home Journal:

"For a month I have been in this city of limited republicanism; this extraordinary example of outward beauty and inward uncleanness; this bewildering cosmopolis of cheap luxuries and expensive necessities; this curious city of contradictions, where you might eat your breakfast from the streets—they are so clean—but

ON THE "BOULE MICHE."

where you must close your eyes to the spectacles of the curbstones; this beautiful whited sepulchre, where exists the unwritten law, 'Commit any offense you will, provided you submerge it in poetry and flowers;' this exponent of outward observances, where a gentleman will deliberately push you into the street if he wishes to pass you in a crowd, but where his action is condoned by his inexpressible manner of raising his hat to you, and the heartfelt sincerity of his apology; where one man will run a mile to restore a lost franc, but if you ask him to change a gold piece he will steal five; where your eyes are ravished with the beauty, and the greenness, and the smoothness and apparent ease of living of all its inhabitants; where your mind is filled with the pictures, the music, the art, the general atmosphere of culture and wit; where the cooking is so good, but so elusive, and where the shops are so bewitching that you have spent your last dollar without thinking, and you are obliged to cable for a new letter of credit from home before you know it—this is Paris."

The young woman who penned those lines may eat her breakfast off the Paris streets if she wants to; I should hate to undertake the contract. In fact, the stories so often told to the effect that a man who throws down a piece of paper, even, in the streets of Paris is at once arrested, and the other narratives as to the fabulous cleanliness of Parisian thoroughfares are simply fairy tales. Still, the system of having the streets washed down by hose attached to hydrants at frequent intervals is an excellent one and might be imitated to advantage in many American cities.

As for learning French, each person must go about it in his or her own way. Dictionaries and phrase books will prove most useful, though the reader will do well to avoid those compiled by foreigners, who are apt to give you this sort of thing:

Que désire monsieur le matin; the café au lait, chocolat?	What do you take in the morning sir; tea, coffee with milke or chocolate?	Ouâte dou zé taike ine zé moruinnque seur: ti, coffi ouise milke or tchoholòte.
Vous m'apporterez le café au lait tous les matins à huit heures.	Bring me coffee witch milk every morning at eight o'clock.	Brinngue mi coffii ouise milke évéri morninngue, it éte o'clock.
C'est entendu monsieur.	Very well sir.	Véry ouel, seur.
UNE CONNAISANCE.	AN ACQUOUAINTANCE	ANEAQUOUAINTANECE
Monsieur est étranger? Oui, monsieur, je suis Anglais.	Are you o foreigner sir? Yes, sir, I am english.	Are you é forineur, seur? Yes, sener, aï ineglíohe.
J'en suis charmé car je tiens tous les Anglais en grande estime.	I am so pleased, because I hold all English people in high esteem.	AÏ ame so slisde, bicause aï holde oll inegliche pepule ine aï estime.
Je vous remercie pour eux.	I thank you in their name.	Aï sannekiou ine sieur nème.
C'est la première fois que vous venez à Paris?	It is the first time you come to Paris	Isite zé feurste taïme, you come tou Pariss.
LA CORRESPONDANCE	THE CORRESPONDANCE	ZÉ CORRESPONDENCE
Donnez moi du papiere à lettre, des enveloppes,	Give me some letter paper, some envelops,	Gnive me some letteur papeur, some envelops,
une plume, un porte-plume,	a pen, a pen handle,	é pène, é pène ha nedeule,
de l'encre, un crayon, une carte postale de dix centimes,	ink, pencil, a post-carde of one penny, fort the city post,	innke, pènecile, é poste carde ove oueune péul for zé citi post,
un timbre de trois sous, un timbre de vingt cinq centimes,	three half penny stamp a two penny half penny stamp,	é tri hafe péni stamp, e tou péni hafe péni stam,
de la cire à cacheter, un cachet pour une lettre chargée.	sealing wax, a seal for a registered letter.	silinngue onâxe, é sile for registeurde litteur.

MAGASIN DE CONFEC-TIONS.	THE READY CLOTHING HOUSE.	ZÉ RÉDY CLOZINNGUE HOUSE.
Bonjour, monsieur, que désirez-vous?	Good morning, sir, what do you desire?	Goud morningne seur oute dou you disaïre?
Je voudrais avoir une veste, un pantalon et un gilet de bonne qualité.	I wan a west, trousers and waistcoat in good marerial.	Aï ouante é vaiste, é traouseurs annde ouèscode in goude matériale.
Nous avons précisément un grand choix en ce moment.	We have just now a large selection.	Oui have djeuste nap é large séléchenne.
Tenez, voici quelque chose de très bon et pas cher.	Here is something very good and not dear.	Hère ise somessinngue véri goude annde note dire.
Combien cela vaut-il?	How much is that worth?	Haouv mentche ise sale oneurste?

These examples I have taken at random from a phrase book picked up in Paris and which many unfortunate Frenchmen use to aid them in acquiring the English language.

One thing is certain, and that is that the best way to learn to speak a language is to speak it. You'll never learn if you are afraid to try to talk. Put yourself as often as possible in places where you've got to talk or get arrested, and never have any false shame or pride about your mistakes. Remember that if your French is broken and your accent as strong as Sandow, the other fellow can't speak English at all.

As to finding your way around Paris and its environs it is too easy. Maps are plentiful and accurate and not dear. One little book, such as the gendarmes and the cab drivers provide themselves with, will prove most useful; it is a street directory of Paris and can be carried in your waistcoat pocket. It tells you where each street begins and where it ends. If you can't get it at Brentano's, 39 Avenue de l'Opera, Pitt & Scott, 9 Rue Scribe will get it for you. As to what you want to see in Paris, either on your bicycle or otherwise, I have nothing to do. Follow your own tastes and any guide book will do the rest. However, for the sake of the ladies, and in no way in the shape of a paid advertisement, I can give them without reservation the address of Madame Herauld, 31 Rue de Douai, Paris, a dressmaker whose work equals that of the Rue de la Paix artists and costs about half as much. Up to date, so far as I know, the clientele is nearly entirely French, which may account for her low prices. It may be well to explain to her that you are cycling, and have seen this notice here. I cannot promise the usual 10 per cent. reduction for cyclists, but I can say that they can go to her with the assurance that she hasn't one set of prices for her French and another for her American customers.

CHAPTER VI.

On An Outing.

LET us assume that you have had enough of Paris, and we'll now plan our first extended bicycle trip. Still, that is badly put. No one ever had enough of Paris, so let us say that having no more time to spend there we have arranged a ride on our wheels from Paris to Venice, taking in the most beautiful part of Switzerland and crossing the Alps en route. As we can't very well describe a trip in advance that we have not taken, perhaps it will be better for us to go over a former trip which I took last September with two married friends of mine, following the exact itinerary. I did not know at the time, and neither did they, that I was going to write anything about it, so it seems unfair that I should drag them into an uncourted notoriety in this connection.

Let us then call them simply Joe and Lou. This much more I will confide to you very quietly: Joe is thirty-five years old, and, being a doctor, tries to look older. Lou is twenty-four, and, being a woman, and not being a doctor, she tries to look younger. She is very jolly, and the only time I saw her look unhappy during the whole trip was in Switzerland; then she confided to me that she had been thinking what a pity it was that she was a blonde instead of a brunette. She would have looked so much better against a background of snow and ice.

It was September 8 when we left Paris, and our friends told us that we were a little late in the season for bicycling in Switzerland. We inclined to that opinion ourselves, and as the weather was not all that it might be, and as the roads within a hundred kilometres of Paris in any direction always leave much to be desired, we drove to the Gare de Lyon and bought tickets to Macon. We took second-class tickets, as every one does in France who has more sense than money. Our tickets cost 33 francs, or $6.60 each, and we had the good fortune to have a compartment to ourselves. For our bicycles we paid two cents. The train left Paris at 2.15 p. m. It was between 7 and 8 o'clock in the evening when we arrived at Dijon, which was the first place at which we had a chance to get anything to eat. The barbarous practice, common with us, of standing at a counter while eating, is unknown in France, even at a railroad restaurant. There were only twenty minutes for refreshments, but the tables were attractively spread for a table d'hote dinner, and were

variously ticketed three and four francs, or sixty and eighty cents, with the wine included. We took a four franc table and Lou worried dreadfully about it. She said she had a great deal too much to eat and wanted to get a rebate, but time wouldn't permit. At 9.40 o'clock we arrived at Macon and drove to the Hotel de l'Europe, which is about ten minutes from the railroad station and on the bank of the river Saone. Our wheels were carefully stowed on top of the omnibus. We found the hotel excellent, and special rates were made for us as soon as it was known that we were cyclists and members of the Touring Club. Joe and Lou paid five francs, or $1, for a great room with two beds. I got one two sizes too big for me for three francs or sixty cents. Lights and service were included. Two beds generally go with all double rooms in French hotels.

The next morning was so mild and the outlook so beautiful that, after crossing the river on the first bridge to the right on leaving the hotel, we rode to Bourg for breakfast. Bourg was thirty kilometres, or a little more than twenty miles, from Macon. We started late, and when we were ready to leave Bourg it was already about 4 o'clock in the afternoon. But with the exhilaration of the wheel strong within us, we were not yet satisfied and decided to keep on to Pont d'Ain, where we were to spend the night in spite of the lowering clouds which threatened rain. We hadn't ridden ten kilometres when it began to rain in good earnest. Ordinarily, under such circumstances, there is some town which will furnish a temporary shelter, or at which you can even put up for the night if the rain continues; but in this case there was nothing between us and our destination. As the rain came down faster and faster we finally decided to take shelter in a little hut with a thatched roof beside of the road.

Here we were made welcome by the old woman in charge, a good type of the French peasant, who seemed very much surprised when she learned that we came from Paris and did not know her daughter Clemence, who was in service there. While we were waiting for the rain to cease the old woman told us that they were all very poor in that neighborhood; they lived on bread and pork, with a potato and a parsnip or two thrown in now and then as a luxury. She said she didn't mind so much in the summer, but in bad weather, during the winter, she and her husband were kept busy shoveling the snow out of the house.

As the rain continued we decided we had better make a move rather than be caught by the darkness as well as the bad weather. Lou was more anxious even than we to move on, and declared that she didn't mind a little wetting, so we set out, and a ride of about three-quarters of an hour brought us to Pont d'Ain, where we went to the Hotel Beau, an unpretentious though excellent hostelry. On our arrival we were

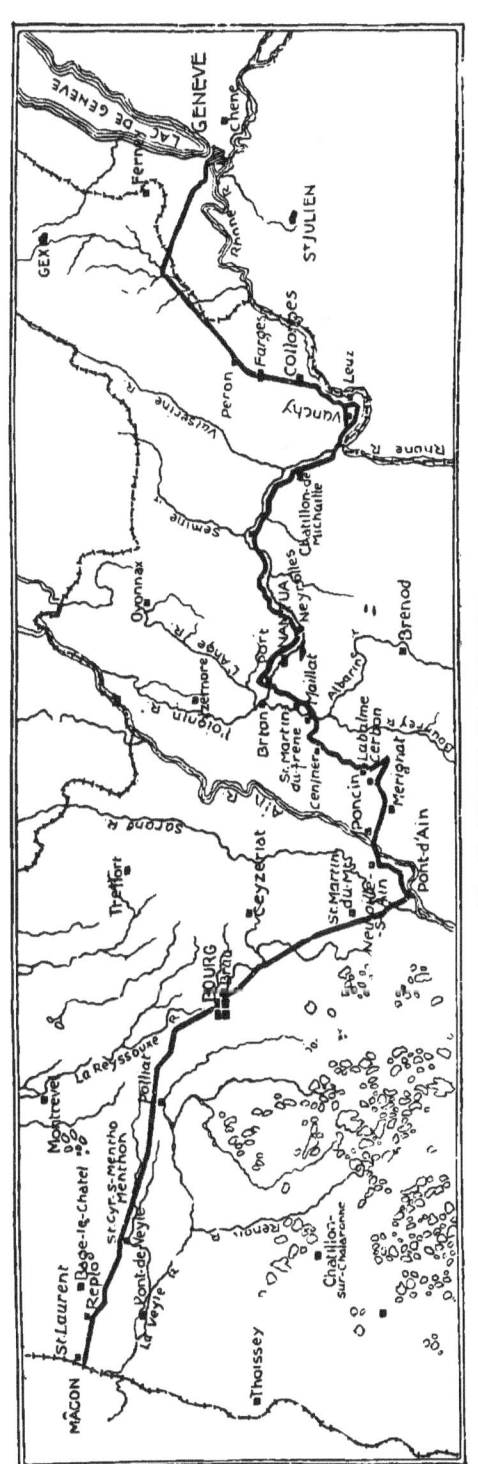

FROM MÂCON TO GENEVA.

pretty wet and our wheels were sights to behold, but, as usual in French towns, there was a mechanic who makes a specialty of looking after bicycles, and we turned them over to his mercies. The house was kept by an old lady with four daughters. They showed us every attention, got dry clothes for Lou, and even got a hot water bottle for her feet. As no such solicitude was shown on our account, Joe and I went out and put a bottle where it would do the most good from our point of view.

The next morning bright and early the bicycle man came around with our machines in excellent order. He charged us a dollar for the three. As it still rained, Joe and I played billiards while Lou wrote letters. If we could have been easily discouraged we would have lost heart right here at the outset of our trip, for it rained steadily two days. But between letter writing and playing cribbage and billiards we managed to pass the time very agreeably, although we were impatient to get on. By the way, if you want to play billiards cheaply go to Pont d'Ain. They don't charge anything there.

On Saturday, September 11, the weather cleared up sufficiently for us to start on our way and we rode on to Cermont, by the way of Poncin, when it began to rain again, and we were driven to the village inn for shelter. We took advantage of the opportunity to order breakfast, during the course of which we learned that our host had been a butler in a Chicago family and had traveled all through the United States. He confided to us that he didn't dare to narrate to his friends in Cermont, where he was born, all the luxuries and comforts of travel and other marvelous things tnat he had seen in America. He said he was afraid if he did he would get the reputation of being the star liar of the district. Early in the afternoon, as the weather nad cleared again, we started out on our way to Nantua, about twenty kilometres further on. Right here let me explain the difference between a kilometre and a mile: A kilometre has 1,000 yards, while, as every schoolboy knows, it takes 1,760 to make a mile. On leaving Cermont one has about six or seven kilometres of hill climbing, but it is the most beautiful hill climbing that can possibly be imagined. As you get up higher and higher, and look back at the little village you are leaving behind you with its picturesque chalets, the rivulets dancing down the mountain side, and the fields below where the cattle browse, with the ever varying shades of light, the effect is marvelous. The road is so tortuous that when you think you have almost come to the end you find yourself at a turn which leads you higher and higher, until you arrive at a point almost opposite that at which you thought you were already nearing the top. In fact the scene is so lovely, and one becomes so lost in the contemplation of it, that one

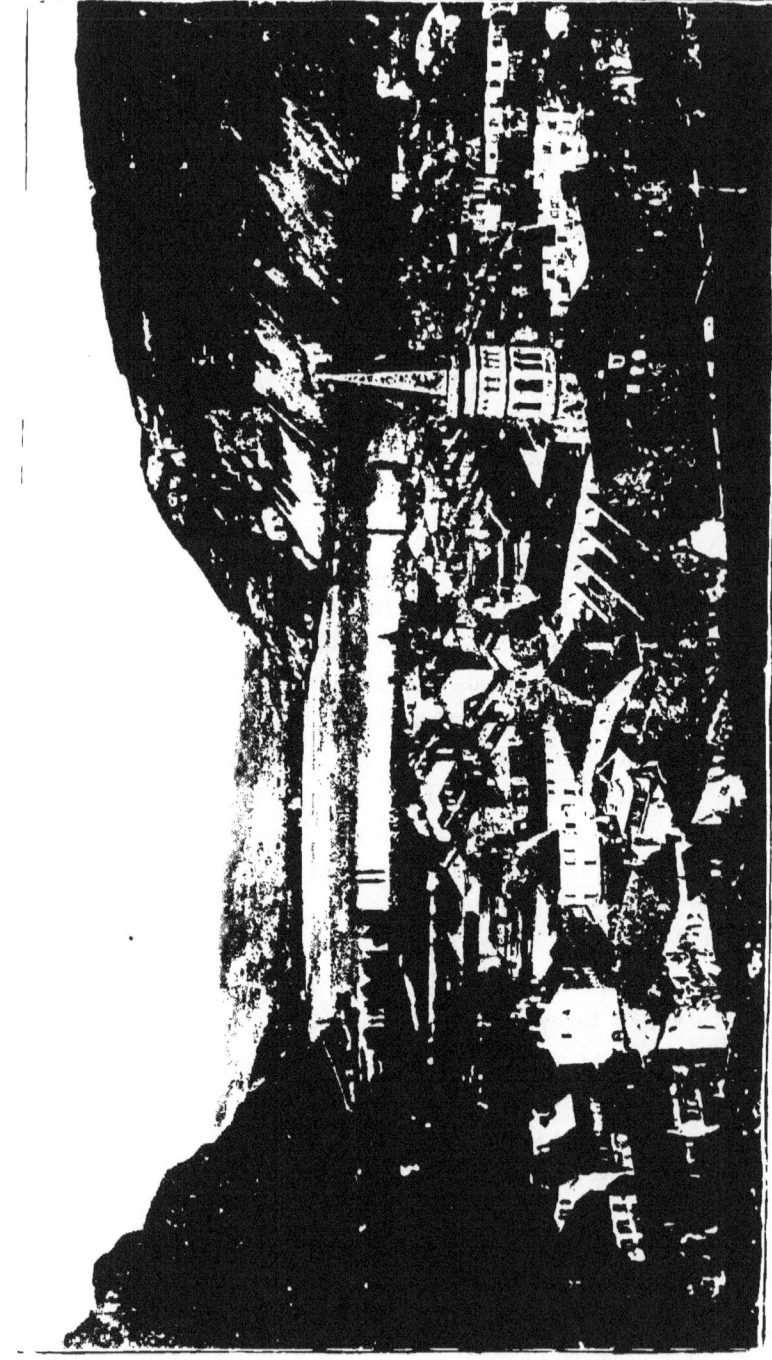

doesn't mind the climbing of the hills at all.

All the way the road is good, and once at the top, one is rewarded with a coast down the other side and a scene almost as beautiful as the panorama on which we had just feasted our eyes. After a ride of ten kilometres a beautiful land-locked lake, nestling in the valley, comes into view, and at the lower end of this there is the town of Nantua. It was nearly 6 o'clock when we rode through the streets of this quaint old town and found excellent quarters at the Hotel de France. Here we remarked that while the rooms were good, they were no better than those we had at Pont d'Ain, although they cost twice as much. Still, that wasn't so much either, as at Pont d'Ain we only paid two francs each for our rooms; Joe and Lou paying no more for their double room than I paid for my single one, an arrangement which obtains very generally in France.

CHAPTER VII.

On to Geneva.

L OU met her first annoyance at Nantua in the morning when she waked up. As usual, she wanted cafe au lait served in her room, but instead of the dainty little service on a tray, the woman appeared with the big coffee pot such as is used down stairs in serving the cafe noir, and seemed much surprised when Lou wanted a little pot of her own. "Why," she said, "just think of what a lot of small pots we would have to have if we served one to each room!" This was only one of many instances we found where the more pretentious the hotel and the more pompous the demeanor of the proprietor the worse the service was. When we got outside the weather was very far from cheering us. It was still raining. However, we borrowed umbrellas and got some fun out of strolling round the town, noticing in the course of our walk that a theatrical troupe was billed to give a performance of the "Courier of Lyons" that evening. The theatre was simply a great tent pitched in an open space in the

middle of the town. Inside the tent there was a very decent arrangement of seats on a rising floor, and the stage was of fair dimensions.

The idea of going to the theatre under such circumstances tickled Lou immensely, and we immediately tried to purchase three reserved seats for the evening. The woman in charge said it was against the rules to sell seats in advance, but good naturedly offered to reserve us three of the best, which we could get and pay for at night. This done, Lou announced that she was going to get her hair shampooed. Meantime, Joe and I got shaved by a barber who said he knew America very well himself, and who wanted to know what part of Brazil we came from. It seems he had passed some time in Rio de Janeiro. It is generally the case in Europe that the distinction between North and South America is very little understood. Meantime, while Lou was getting her hair dried, Joe and I played billiards, and by this time we were ready for breakfast, which was very bountiful, and, as usual, included wine. The price of the breakfast was three francs, which, unlike the general custom, was the same price as the dinner. The dinner was also very good, though, as in so many other French hotels, there was a great deal too much of it. Our rooms at this hotel for four francs were fair and Joe and Lou paid no more than I did.

In the evening an agreeable surprise awaited us; I have seen very much less meritorious performances of well known plays given in fair sized American cities than that of the "Courier of Lyons" as presented by the French troupe in that big tent at Nantua. In fact, so good was their work, and so strange did it seem to see such unusual talent under such odd conditions, that when it rained the following day, which was Saturday, we didn't know whether to be disappointed or to be glad, for it gave us a chance to stay longer and see the same company give a performance of "La Fille de Madame Angot," which they did with a tunefulness and a go simply refreshing. They also numbered in their repertoire such pieces as "La Perichole," "Le Petit Duc" and "Madame Sans Gene," and many others equally ambitious.

That night the company was billed in "Le Petit Duc," but as it still rained, and as we were not particularly pleased with the hotel, in spite of the length of its menu, we took a train toward 6 o'clock for Bellegarde, some twenty-five kilometres further on in our journey. We disliked to do this, because the road between Nantua and Bellegarde is very good, and from what we saw of it from the train the scenery must be beautiful. At Bellegarde we went to the Hotel des Touristes, which is kept by two sisters, who were extremely agreeable. We had been advised not to go to this hotel, as the proprietor of it had been murdered by one of his servants about six months before, and this fact was supposed to cast a hoodoo over the house and all who went there. We consulted Lou on the subject, and she said she just doted on hoodoos and wouldn't hear of going anywhere else. Joe and Lou got an excellent room for four francs, while I had good quarters for two francs fifty centimes or fifty cents.

Incidentally, Lou ascertained that the maid of all work received for her services the munificent sum of $4 per month, and was expected to be up shortly after four o'clock in the morning and not to go to bed before ten. Lou said she had rather ride a bicycle.

At last, on September 13, the sun consented to smile on our little expedition, and we set out about eleven o'clock for Chancy, a town on the frontier, between France and Switzerland. We had decided to take our dejeuner a la fourchette at Collonges, a little more than twenty kilometres away. The ride to this place was delightful. At first it was up a continuous ascent, some of which is too steep to ride comfortably, though most of it can be negotiated without effort. In fact, Lou could take hills quite as well as we could. She said it was because she didn't smoke. The road was in excellent condition, and as you ride along you get a magnificent view of the gorge below, through which flow narrow streams of water which sparkle in the sunlight, being fed from the mountain brooks dancing down the mountain side to our left and passing through waterways made for them under the road along which we were wheeling.

Far, far below, too, on the further side of the gorge, were two railroad tracks, and every now and then we could see trains in motion, so far away that they seemed to be only crawling along, and it was interesting to see them disappear into some tunnel of great length, oftentimes dug through solid rock, only to appear again at the other end, their coming being heralded by little puffs of smoke.

When we got to Collonges we were nearly up to the top of our climb. We breakfasted in the funniest of little road-side inns, where the natives must have mighty appetites, judging from the supply of viands set before us. As usual, the breakfast included wine, and cost us fifty cents apiece. After breakfast we were very glad to soon find ourselves riding down a hill toward Chancy.

We bowled at great speed, and in wonderful spirits, across the bridge at Chancy, when suddenly a man stepped out of a little house, at the right of the road, and held up his hands for us to stop. We understood in a moment what he meant. We were about to cross our first frontier, and that was his way of telling us to stand and deliver. Lou said afterwards that she knew she could have ridden by him and he could never have touched her. As a matter of fact, I have no doubt she could have done so, and it would often be possible to cross a frontier in this way, but it would never be advisable. If one should undertake to do such a thing the official would simply telephone or telegraph to other officials along the route which you would have to take and you would be sure to be held up, and the consequences of your indiscretion might be serious.

As it was we all dismounted, and as we were each armed with our cards of identification as members of the French Touring Club, we expected no trouble whatever. The Swiss officials were very polite, and after having carefully examined my card and that of Joe, and having compared the name of the maker and the number on the card with the name and the number on the machine, they pronounced them all right and said we might proceed.

Whether Lou had brought along the hoodoo from that hotel at Bellegarde or not I cannot say, but trouble began at once when she handed over her card of identity. The official examined it carefully, looked puzzled, smiled a little, and then looked at Lou curiously.

"Guess he thinks I'm smuggling something," said Lou, sotto voce, in English.

We could not understand what was the trouble, for her card was identical with our own. Then the official proceeded to explain, pointing out the fact, that while Lou's card was en regle in all other respects it lacked the number.

"But the machine has no number," Joe exclaimed.

"But it should have," said the Swiss official. "I never saw one before that didn't have."

Now the fact was that Lou had learned to ride a bicycle in the Bois de Vincennes, near Nogent Vincennes, and had let the man of whom she hired the wheel, and who took charge of her instruction, build her a bicycle to order, from the parts of machines which he had received from England. Not being a bicycle manufacturer, and never having put together more than half a dozen machines in his life, he had never bothered about numbering them.

We explained this to our Swiss friend with all the gentleness possible, but he would not have it.

"You gentlemen can go on," he said, "but the lady cannot cross this frontier."

"Do you mean to say that we have got to go back to Paris to have the man who made the machine put on a number?" we asked.

"No," he said, "you can have the number put on anywhere in France.

"Will any old number do?" asked Joe.

"Certainly," said the Cerberus of the Swiss frontier. "All you have to do is to take this machine somewhere on your side of the frontier and have it numbered; then come back here and the lady can go on with you."

On inquiry, he informed us that there was a blacksmith's shop he thought about two kilometres back on the way we had come. Seeing that there was nothing for it but to comply with this seemingly ridiculous requirement, we mounted our machines and turned back, although the sky was growing overcast again. Lou never said a word for the first kilometre, then turning to us, she ejaculated, "Will you two swear for me, please?" We complied with pleasure.

We found the blacksmith's shop without trouble, but as often with French workingmen, the proprietor was not at work. His wife was there, however, along with five or six dirty children. After some difficulty we persuaded the woman to crawl into the shop through a window and bring out as many sharp pointed tools as she could get hold of. With one of these instruments Joe went to work to try to cut a number on Lou's machine. He could make little impression on the hard frame with the comparatively dull instrument he had to work with, but he finally did succeed in cutting a pretty fair imitation of the number 13 on the enamel surface of both the front and back part of the frame of the machine.

But this didn't suit Lou. She might dote on hoodoos in a general way, but she was not going to ride a machine numbered 13. Thereupon Joe added another three to the numbers already cut, and having tipped the old lady, we all started merrily back to Chancy. Lou's machine, which had caused so much suspicion when it was unnumbered, now passed muster all right with those magic symbols 133, and the Swiss official sent us on our way rejoicing. Meantime, the clouds, which had long been threatening, began to drip rain, and when we were still eighteen kilometres from Geneva, we found ourselves caught in a nasty drizzle storm. We had begun to think that we were in for another ride in the wet, and Lou was remarking on the difficulty of keeping her hair in crimp, when we saw a tram car by the side of the road. We asked the conductor where it went, and to our delight learned that it went right into the heart of Geneva, and that if we wanted to take it there was plenty of room on the front platform for our bicycles.

In an hour we were in Geneva, and as the rain had ceased falling, we got on our machines and started to ride through the town. We did this in accordance with an invariable rule which we followed all through the trip, and which, undoubtedly, saved us a great deal of money. We would never decide beforehand what hotel we would go to before arriving at any given place.

CHAPTER VIII.

Adventures in Geneva.

IN THIS way we were able to ride around the town and look over the various hotels to suit ourselves. If we saw one which was not too pretentious, and yet appeared to be to our liking, we would ride up to it, dismount, lean our wheels against a convenient tree or place them in the racks usually provided for bicycles, and then order some refreshments, as if we had not the slightest idea of taking rooms there. A little later we would ask the waiter casually if they had rooms to let, and how the prices ranged. Within a few moments that waiter was sure to have the master or mistress of the establishment out on the sidewalk, and it was equally certain that the proprietor would make us the most alluring terms, fearing that we would ride away without inspecting the rooms. If the prices were reasonable, Lou would go in and see if the accommodations were suitable, and there we were, settled without any bother or embarrassment or haggling about rates. The advantage of this mode of procedure is obvious. If you ride up to a hotel with the avowed intention of staying there, before you have a chance of making any arrangements the porters and waiters have grabbed your bicycles, unstrapped your baggage, and probably stowed away the whole outfit in some back room, then feeling already half sure of their prey, the patron piles on the price. Having gone so far, you feel embarrassed about going, and even if you do so, all the employees will expect tips for having handled your machines.

In Geneva, of course, there is no lack of hotels, and many of them are of high grade and not dear from the American standpoint. Four dollars a day would probably cover all your expenses at any of them. But we thought that we could do better, and events proved that we were right. After riding around for an hour we came to the conclusion that most of the people of Geneva were trying to support themselves by renting rooms. There were signs of rooms or apartments to let, of every description, on all sides and in all parts of the city..

At the end of our hour's ride we found ourselves very comfortably located in rooms up one flight, in a house where furnished rooms were to let without board. We never went to boarding houses. The rooms were very agreeable, and situated near the grounds of the late exposition. When we left Macon we had sent our trunks by grande vitesse, to meet us at

Geneva. We had no difficulty whatever in getting them here. We merely gave the keys to a man employed in the house and we had them the next morning. We had taken them as far as Macon with us because our tickets to that place entitled us to that amount of baggage, and it was cheaper to express them on from there to Geneva than it would have been from Paris. The price of the rooms which we engaged was no higher than that which we had been paying.

Joe and Lou paid four francs for their room, and were blessed with the liberal supply of three beds. Joe said that Lou put her bicycle in the third bed every night, but Lou denied it. My room cost me three francs and only had one bed. I don't think that was quite fair, but didn't say anything, as sixty cents a day isn't so very dear for a room one flight up with a bed eight feet wide. We were also able to make special arrangements by which Lou could get tea or coffee and bread and butter in her room every morning for one franc. When we asked what the weather outlook was we were told that it was good, because it had already been raining at Geneva for a week. That night we dined at the Cafe Lyrique, near the Theatre Lyrique. This is an excellent cafe, the portions being large even from an American point of view, and the prices were reasonable. By the way, if you drink wine, every one will be advising you to try a brand called Asti. All I can say is, don't do it. Maple syrup is sour by comparison. That night we were tired and went to bed, only to get up and find it still raining. We made a trip around town, though, and in searching for a restaurant at which to breakfast, we were directed to the Hotel du Nord.

We had an excellent breakfast at this restaurant, and there is no question that the chef understands his business, but the prices are higher even than at a similar place in Paris. The check was for twenty-four francs and we didn't have much either.

Outside, Lou complained of indigestion; she said she didn't know whether it was the breakfast or the check.

That night we went to a real theatre, the only one open at the time in Geneva. They were playing "Charley's Aunt" or "La Marraine de Charley," as it is known in the French version. It wasn't badly done, but Lou said she didn't enjoy it half as much as the performances in that tent at Nantua.

We had now got to September 16 and the weather was still gloomy, yet it didn't rain. In a spasm of economy and still remembering the check for twenty-four francs at the Hotel du Nord, Lou dragged us to some place where we could breakfast for 30 cents. I had rather not say much about that breakfast, but it certainly wasn't worth more than they asked for it. After breakfast, while Lou went home to put on her bicycle costume, Joe and I went and got something to eat. That afternoon we rode all over Geneva, although the roads outside of the city were still in such a condition as to make it impossible for us to continue our journey. It is remarkable how much more of a city you can see in one afternoon on a bicycle than you possibly could in traveling around a number of days on foot. I need not tell you of the myriad of pretty articles in the way of jewelry and souvenirs displayed in the show windows at Geneva. When you get there you will see them for yourself.

On September 17 we called on the United States Consul at Geneva, Benjamin H. Ridgely, who, besides being an authority on international law and a linguist who speaks French as well as he does English, is an enthusiastic cyclist. Mr. Ridgely has made the tour of the Lake of Geneva on his wheel more than a dozen times, besides having ridden over most of Southern Europe. To him we are indebted for the route which we subsequently took on our trip to Interlaken and across the Alps to Milan and Venice. He also kindly lent us some maps of his own which were invaluable to us on the journey. Mr. Ridgely expressed the opinion that the trip from Brigue across the Simplon to Domo d'Ossola is perhaps the most beautiful bicycle ride in the world.

That afternoon Joe had an adventure which illustrates a curious practice in Switzerland. Joe speaks French pretty well, so when he went into a barber shop he said with calm confidence,

"La barbe, une seule fois, bien vite s'il vous plait," meaning to say, "Shave, once over, mighty quick, please."

To Joe's surprise the man grabbed the scissors and began to make frantic attempts to cut his hair. Joe flushed a little to think his French should meet with such a reception. Hastily he seized a razor in his hand and said again, in French, "What's the matter with you? I said shave."

At last the man, seeing the razor, seemed to comprehend, and proceeded to shave his victim.

When he was through Joe said very distinctly "Pas de poudre," naturally wishing to say "no powder," whereupon the man seized the puff and powdered Joe vigorously all over the face, not missing his mouth when Joe opened it to expostulate.

"Don't you speak French?" cried Joe. "Nein," said the man with a stupid look.

Joe began to think he was in an idiot asylum when the proprietor came out of the back room and offered this explanation. His employe, he said, was what is known in Switzerland as a Volontaire, that is to say, he was one of those Germans who come over into a French Canton to learn the French language, offering his services voluntarily and receiving only his board for his work.

But Joe's saddest adventure in Geneva was of a more serious character. The night before the last of our stay there we dined at the Grand

Cafe. I had walked down with Lou, and Joe was the only one with a bicycle. When we started to go home it was raining a little and Joe asked the proprietor if he could leave his bicycle at the cafe. That gentleman said "certainly," and was greatly insulted when Joe wanted to put his chain on it. "Your bicycle is as safe here as it would be in your own house," he said with a grandiloquent air. So Joe did not insist further, but left his wheel, with some misgivings.

Next morning Joe called and got his wheel. On mounting it he noticed that the hind tire bumped. Getting off, he found the tire entirely deflated, and looking for the cause, found a nail in it more than an inch long. He dragged the proprietor out to look at it. That individual was very sorry, but he had merely promised Joe that his wheel would be safe, and the only thing he could imagine was that one of the members of his orchestra must have taken it out for an early morning ride, and that after having picked up the nail, must have ridden back with the air out of the tube. There was nothing for Joe to do but go to the representatives of the manufacturer of his tire at Geneva. There they tried to repair the tire but the cut was so near the valve, they said, that when it was blown up it exploded, and Joe had to buy another tire of the same make. The manufacturers of the tire at Paris subsequently sent him a new tire without charge on his representation of the case. The tire reached us at Milan.

The night of September 21 was bright and starlight, so we made arrangements for the forwarding of our trunks to Interlaken, and prepared to continue our journey next morning.

CHAPTER IX.

En Route at Last.

O N the morning of September 21 we realized the truth of the proverb which runs as the French put it, "Tout vient a point a qui sait attendre." Surely we had waited long enough for the sun, and, at length, there it was in all its glory. Our next step may seem singular to most cyclists, for instead of riding to Lausanne we took the lake steamer which left the Quai du Mont-Blanc at about eleven o'clock. It is true that the roads were perfectly rideable, and that a tour even around the whole of Lake Geneva is a most interesting one. At the same time, on such a trip as we were undertaking, one gets plenty of bicycling, and by taking a steamer we had a chance to see both sides of the lake, as the boat touches here and there at ports on either shore; whereas had we ridden to Lausanne, we would have only seen the lake from one side. Besides we were able to breakfast very comfortably on board and found the cuisine excellent.

The following is an account of an excursion

around the lake from a local publication:

"This beautiful excursion is generally made on the spacious steamboat called La Suisse, which leaves the Quai du Mont-Blanc at 9 o'clock in the morning and returns to Geneva at 8 o'clock. Return tickets are issued for this excursion. There is an excellent restaurant on board where dinner may be had at any time.

"The steamboat follows at first the Swiss side of the lake, passing before Coppet, where there is the chateau of Madame de Stael, Nyon, a little town in the Canton de Vaud containing a picturesque chateau; a little further on, at Prangins, there is the house and estate which belonged to Prince Napoleon. The boat now crosses the lake and touches at Thonon and Evian from where it again returns to the Swiss side and stops at Ouchy (funicular tramway up to Lausanne). Continuing along the Swiss side of the lake, the steamer passes before Vevey, Montreux, le Chateau de Chillon and stops at Villeneuve. During the whole of this part of the sail visitors will be able to admire the superb mountains which surround the lake, the Dents d'Oche, the Cornettes de Bise, the Grammont, and farther back the Dent du Midi with its seven points.

"This excursion may also be made in another way. The express boat may be taken at 6 o'clock, at half-past ten the visitor will be at Territet, where he may take the funicular railway up to Glion and from there the coggedwheel railway up to the top of the Rochers de Naye, at an altitude of about 2,044 metres, or about 6,800 feet, where he will arrive at 12 o'clock. The view is superb and the way up most interesting. At 2 o'clock the train must be taken again down to Territet, from where La Suisse starts at 3:30, arriving at Geneva at 8 o'clock."

There is no use to attempt to describe the beauties of the scenery by which Lake Geneva is environed. It is known as one of the most beautiful lakes in the world, and the scene from the boat was such a lovely one that Lou declared she believed even the bicycles enjoyed it. It was still early in the afternoon when we arrived at Ouchy. As soon as we were fairly on shore we mounted our bicycles and, instead of climbing up the steep hill which leads to Lausanne, we set out on the road which winds along the shore of the lake and, exhilarated by the air of a perfect September day, wheeled along at a pace which we would never have dared to touch during the epoch of cloudy weather and muddy roads which we had so far experienced.

Our destination now was Montreux, which is known as the Nice of Switzerland. The further we rode the more delightful the scenery became. To our left were sunny slopes covered with vines heavy with ripening grapes of both the light and dark varieties. To the right, at our feet, were the pellucid waters of the lake with their peculiar blue, and further ahead and to the right again, were snow-capped mountains which seemed in the sharper contrast from the rich verdure and ruddy grapes about us. We arrived at Montreux about six o'clock in the evening.

The only thing which provoked Lou during the trip was the fact that she couldn't get any milk that was not boiled. The idea that one must drink boiled milk or none at all was too much for her. When we didn't seem to sympathize enough with her she said she guessed we would appreciate the situation better if we couldn't get anything but boiled absinthe or boiled beer. Even at Vevey, a popular winter resort for foreigners, Lou was equally unfortunate in her attempt to get fresh milk. At Montreux we went to the Hotel du Parc, where we had an excellent table d'hote at three francs each, and wine included. Our rooms afforded an excellent view of the scenery for which Montreux is famous, but owing to the popularity of the place as a winter resort prices ran a little higher than usual, Joe and Lou paying five francs for their room while I got off for four.

It had been our intention to ride on from here to Fribourg, but when we learned that every bit of the way was up hill and that even the trains required two engines to pull them up the incline we decided to take the train ourselves, as it was only a matter of something more than thirty kilometers and the fare was insignificant.

A REFRESHING SWISS WATERFALL.

The fact was Lou had confided to Joe that she was afraid she would get bow-legged if she walked up too many hills, and Joe, who was getting a little stout, was quite as ready to ride as she was, though he made her believe that he only consented as a great personal sacrifice.

If there had been a person of average intelligence at Montreux we would have been obliged to ride back only as far as Chexbres, just the other side of Vevey, in order to take the train which passed through there for Fribourg about three o'clock in the afternoon. But as it was we were told we would have to ride away back to Lausanne over the road which we had come in order to get a train which went to Fribourg. This train left Lausanne a little after two o'clock and was the one we might have taken at Chexbres, if they had only known enough to tell us about it. It wasn't that we minded going over that route again, but the difficulty came after we arrived at Ouchy, where to reach Lausanne we had to climb a hill practically impossible to ride, being steep and about six kilometers long. As we were ascending the hill a woman driving a horse attached to a sort of buckboard and which, by the constant use of the whip, she kept at a lively trot, became so lost to everything else in her contemplation of Lou that she nearly ran over that young woman, much to the latter's indignation. Once at the top of the hill at Lausanne one is rewarded by a view for which Lou could find no other expression than "Simply gorgeous!" Still we were getting so used to lovely views that it is doubtful whether we would have climbed that hill for this particular one if we'd known about the station at Chexbres. As we had more than an hour on our hands before train t.me we went to the Hotel Terminus for our breakfast.

On adding up the check Joe noticed that the waiter had charged us one franc each for our coffee and cognac, though it should not by any possibility have been more than ten cents or, at most, twelve cents. Joe questioned the waiter and then asked the head waiter about the charge. Both insisted that it was all right, and to the astonishment of Lou and myself Joe paid the check without further expostulation. As soon as we were off the porch Lou turned to her husband and said: "Can we never make a traveler of you? Why that was simply extortion."

"Never mind, my dear," said Joe, quietly, showing the check. "God has punished the wicked head waiter; he forgot to mark the bottle of wine we had."

It was a fact; in their haste to charge double price for the coffee and cognac they had forgotten to mark down our bottle of wine which, if I remember rightly, was three francs. Anyway it was a case of the biter bit.

Our tickets to Fribourg were something like five francs each and as, drawn by two engines, the train puffed slowly up the incline we had almost as good a chance to view the scenery as we would have had if we had been pushing our bicycles on foot, particularly as we had one of those cars so often found in Switzerland in which one can walk from one end to the other. At Fribourg we merely made a brief tour of the town on our bicycles, as Joe had conceived the idea of getting to a little Swiss hamlet called Noreaz. This place was the home of an old and faithful Swiss valet who had served his family a long time on both sides of the Atlantic. He was at present home on a vacation and Joe had promised him that if he ever rode through Switzerland he would look him up. We learned that Noreaz was only about 15 kilometers from Fribourg and rode there over a series of most picturesque by-paths which may never before have known the mark of a foreigner's wheel. As we approached Noreaz, which is prettily situated half way up the low mountain, our ears were greeted by the sound of most peculiar music.

"It sounds like a xylophone," I ventured.

"It is the Angelus," said Lou in an awed tone.

"It's cows," said Joe. And Joe was right.

As we rounded a sharp turn there in the meadow below were at least a hundred cattle gathered in for the night. Each one wore a bell and each bell was of a different size and attuned to a different key. The effect was really like that of many sets of chimes rung together, so Lou's mistake was not at all an unnatural one.

Our arrival at Noreaz, a place of some one hundred and twenty inhabitants, created a veritable sensation not unmixed with consternation, if one may judge by the fact that one boy dropped a pail of milk and another fell into the watering trough just at the sight of Lou. They had never seen a woman cyclist before. But as for Eugene, the faithful dependent whom we had come to look up, he was at once astonished and overjoyed, and nothing would do but that we must come with him and break bread and drink wine under the family roof. It was now too late for us to get back to Fribourg that night so we were lodged in the little chalet which served as an inn. The rooms were so low that one couldn't jump for joy without danger of a fractured skull, but the roof we felt quite certain would stay on during the night at least, because it was held down by several monster rocks. Lou said she didn't care whether it blew off or not as she always had a weakness for astronomy and star-gazing generally. The view from the chalet was superb, or at least as much of it as we could see through the lilliputian windows.

All Noreaz had gathered at our door the following morning to see us start back on our way to Fribourg, to which place we were obliged to return before setting out for Berne, about thirty kilometers from Fribourg. Fribourg, as I have already said, is only fifteen kilometers from Noreaz, leaving us only about forty-five kilometers for the day, about Lou's size, although frequently she didn't mind sixty, and once later on in Holland, even so far forgot herself as to ride one hundred without noticing it. We found Fribourg in gala attire. The whole population had turned out to attend the trial of a man who had murdered the station master of a nearby town. Fribourg is an interesting city with a very old cathedral, which Lou wouldn't go into, however, declaring she had rather miss a picture or two than get a cold in the head. By the way, if you happen to have anybody in your path in life and want to get rid of him, just get him to cycle with you in Europe during the hot weather and then push him into two or three old cathedrals as you go by, while you stay outside yourself.

The suspension bridge at Fribourg is regarded as a great engineering feat and one of the sights of the city. We had to cross it on our way to Berne and found the view on the middle of it very fine.

Once over the bridge and up a short hill to the left we found the road to Berne excellent, though the scenery wasn't particularly interesting. One thing we noticed in this district, and in fact nearly everywhere throughout Switzerland, was the great number of women and children working in the fields. Very few men were visible. At Berne we first went to a hotel marked in the book as the Touring Club of France as one on its list. Here we were un-

CROSSING THE BRIDGE AT FRIBOURG.

able to follow our usual tactics as there were no tables outside. However, I stayed with the bicycles in the courtyard while Joe and Lou went up to look at the room. The name of the hotel was the Hotel du Falcon and when Joe and Lou came down they were unanimous that they wouldn't have the room at any price. No attempt was made to prevent our exit, though the proprietor from the moment he learned our decision treated us with great hauteur. It was now quite dark and it was drizzling outside so we were ready to take almost anything that might offer for the night, but fortunately tumbled on the Hotel Pfistern, or Hotel des Boulangers, as it is also known. This proved to be one of the best hotels we had found yet, though a little higher priced than many. We paid six and four francs respectively for our rooms. The restaurant was extremely good and the prices were not too high.

Lou said she would hate to be in the umbrella trade in Berne, and we agreed with her. One can walk up and down the sidewalks of almost any of the streets of Berne in the business part of the town, even when it is raining hard, without getting in the least wet. The upper part of the houses are built out over the sidewalks so that one walks along a continuous arcade on the inner side of which are the shop windows, while in the archways which occur every few feet are open counters and tables covered with every knick-knack and gew-gaw peculiar to the country.

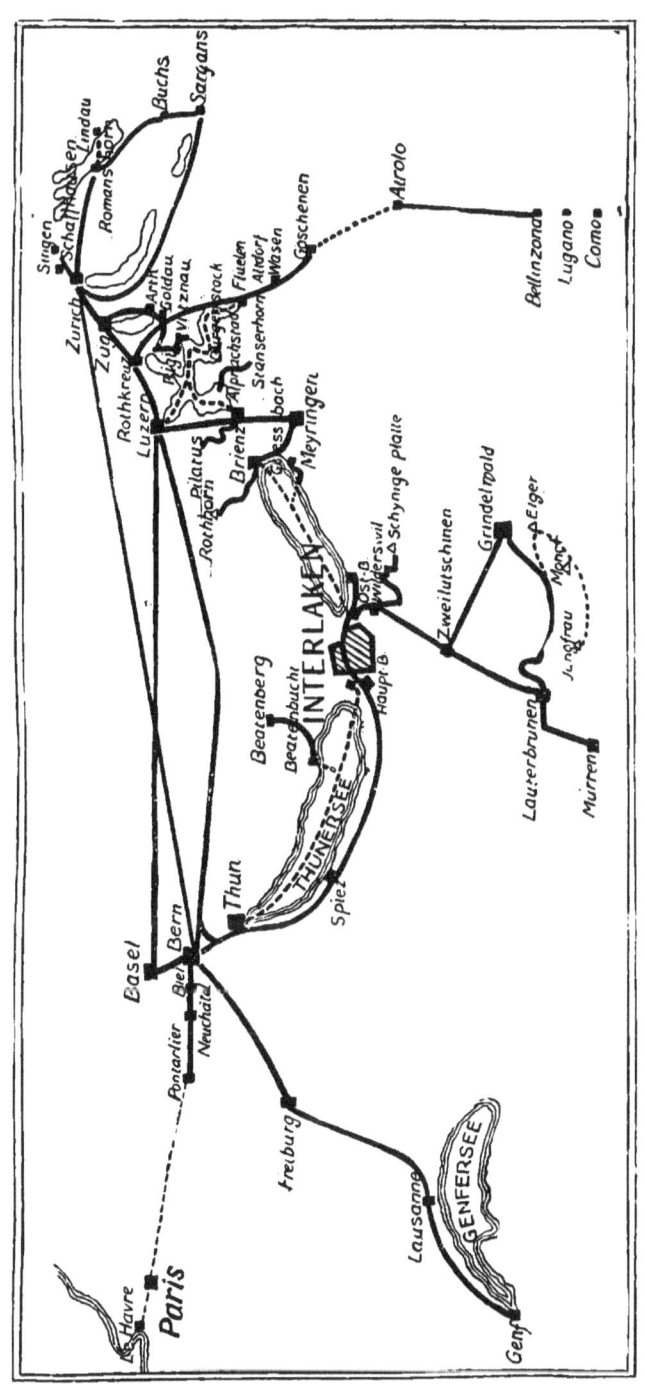

FROM BERN TO MEYRINGEN.

One of the interesting sights of Berne is the clock tower with a clock which strikes every quarter of an hour. From the suspension bridge one has an excellent view of the Jungfrau. Then, of course, Berne wouldn't be Berne without its bear pit, which has existed there for many, many generations until the bears have become much more important in Berne than the aldermen are at New York. It is really doubtful whether Berne could get along without her bears, while New York—but never mind that. One thing we all noticed about Berne was its unusual number of really handsome women. In fact, we saw more good-looking women there than anywhere else on any of our tours. They were not only fine looking but of superb physique and brimming over with health and spirits. Lou said that she has a suspicion that that is why we found Berne interesting enough to keep us there three days in spite of fine weather. But then, Lou doesn't mean all that she says.

The guide book states that ninety-five per cent. of the inhabitants of Berne are German and that only five per cent. speak French. If this is the case we must have met someone who belonged to that five per cent. whenever, as frequently happened, we were obliged to enquire our way or seek other information; for nearly every well-dressed person whom we accosted spoke at least a little French, and in one or two instances we met natives who were anxious

A SCENE IN THE OBERLAND BERNOIS.

to try their alleged English on us. At last we managed to tear ourselves away from Berne with its bears and other manifold attractions, and set out for Thun, an interesting old town at the head of Lake Thun, only thirty kilometers away. The road was very direct and the wheeling good, though there was nothing particularly thrilling in the scenery.

On arriving at Thun we gave our bicycles into the charge of the bicycle dealer of the town to be thoroughly cleaned and looked over generally. We found very good quarters at the Hotel Freienhof, near what is known as the Jardin Anglais. Joe's room cost the usual five francs, while I got off for three; the table d'hote dinner cost only two francs each. The next morning there was so much delay in getting our bill ready that we took all our baggage and went to the place where we had left our bicycles. There was nothing to prevent our leaving without settling with our host but that fact didn't disturb him in the least, and it is true that in nearly any part of Europe American and English tourists share the confidence of tradesmen and hotel people to a degree that native customers can never hope to enjoy. After we had gone back and settled our bill we set out for Interlaken along the upper or left hand side of the lake of Thun, going towards that place. Here we were most agreeably surprised by a bit of landscape which had not perhaps been equaled since we began our ride.

The road all along the way was perfect for wheeling; with the exception of one hill which we had to climb it was mostly down grade. At places the road was almost entirely overhung with great crags and ledges of rock, and every now and then our way led through tunnels cut through the rocks sometimes a hundred yards in length. These holes through bits of mountain must have been dug at great expense but were made absolutely necessary by the character of the country. They were invariably dripping with moisture and quite dark in the middle. At first we approached them with caution and no little anxiety but after having passed several and found the road bed secure we rode with more confidence. To leave the warm sunshine outside, disappear into one of these subterranean passages only to emerge into the daylight at the other end, gave one a very odd but quite enjoyable sensation. In fact, I think we all remembered that ride from Thun to Interlaken, after the trip was over, as one of our jolliest experiences. We wheeled into Interlaken shortly after four o'clock in the afternoon. It was on the 26th of September and as that happened to be Sunday the streets were filled with merry-makers, who were only too glad to enjoy the perfect weather after the rains which had prevailed earlier in the month.

CHAPTER X.

Across the Grimsel.

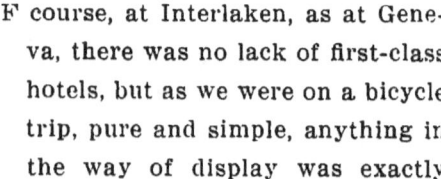

OF course, at Interlaken, as at Geneva, there was no lack of first-class hotels, but as we were on a bicycle trip, pure and simple, anything in the way of display was exactly what Lou wanted to avoid. Therefore, according to our custom, we rode about the town for an hour or so, stopping at the cafes of several hotels before we finally made our selection. The hotel we picked out as the result of our investigation was the Hotel Bernerhof, where we got rooms affording us an excellent view of the Jungfrau. At this hotel we made an arrangement differing a little from our usual plan. We were to have our rooms with the cafe au lait served in them, together with a table d'hote dinner at night, with wine. Our solid breakfast, or dejeuner a la fourchette, we were to take a la carte, either at the hotel or elsewhere as we pleased. This enabled us to ride out after cafe au lait and take breakfast anywhere we liked without being obliged to pay for another at the hotel. This made our expenses individ-

ADJACENT MOUNTAINS.

OUR HOTEL AT INTERLAKEN.

ually less than eight francs a day, with everything included, which, besides being very cheap for Interlaken, gave us absolute freedom as to our movements. The proprietor of the hotel spoke both French and English.

The Sunday night of our arrival we went to the Kursaal, where we listened to excellent music, besides doing a little mild gambling at a game something on the order of the petits chevaux except that a little railroad train, instead of the horses, runs around the circle and stops at one of the stations marked on the board. These stations bear the names of the principal capitals of Europe, and as there are eight of them, and as you are only paid six for one in case you happen to guess rightly which station the train is going to stop at, it will be readily seen that it is a hard game to beat.

The next morning we spent in mousing around Interlaken, where Lou picked up lots of little trinkets in the way of souvenirs. When Lou began to buy things it was always a matter of congratulation to Joe that she was traveling on a bicycle and couldn't carry much with her. In the afternoon we rode on our wheels to Lauterbrunnen through the mysterious valley entirely shut in by mountains, to get a glimpse of the famous waterfall, an unceasing stream pouring over the picturesque cliff on the mountain above the road. Here again we got the effect of that same weird music which had attracted our attention at Noreaz; but this time

PICTURESQUE STAUBACH FALLS.

the bells were attached to goats, not to cattle. The road to Lauterbrunnen is only a little more than fifteen kilometers, and if one does have to climb a slight rise all the way in getting there, one has a glorious coast back. The next day we had planned to go and visit one of the glaciers on the Jungfrau. To do this we bought tickets to Grindewald. The tickets cost only something like 60 cents and the distance was only twenty-three kilometers, though it takes the train about two hours to make the trip. Of course anyone could ride on one's wheel to Grindewald, but I should advise against doing so, for, besides arriving in a heavy perspiration, the system could not fail to be more or less exhausted after that hard and continuous ascent, and one would be in no condition to take the walk over the snow and ice of the glacier, and penetrate the great ice cave cut nearly a hundred yards through the solid ice of the glacier. Therefore, we went by train, and at Grindewald took horses and a guide for our visit to the grotto with its mysterious recesses and weird echoes, and later to the lower glacier and that wondrous cave through the solid ice. This is a most enjoyable trip and should not be missed by anyone who goes to Interlaken. As for Lou, she was perfectly delighted and declared if she ever rode horseback again she would do it in her bicycle costume. The guide and two horses cost Joe sixteen francs. I preferred to walk. This price was a little lower than usual as the season was over.

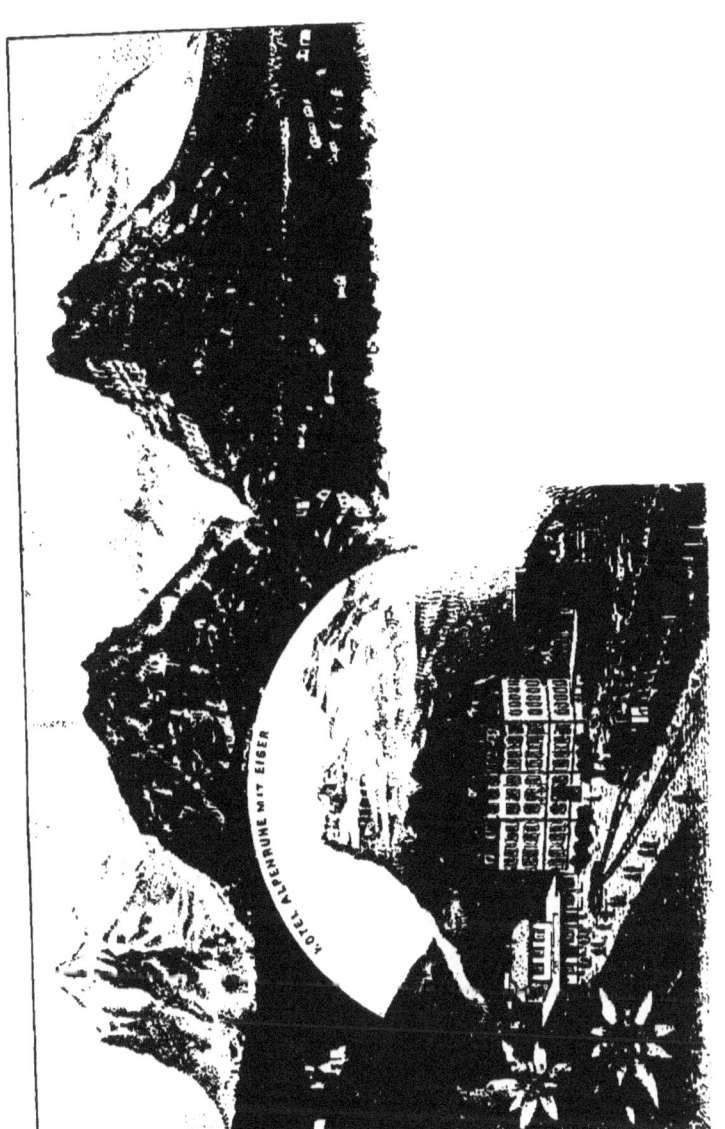

WHERE YOU TAKE HORSES TO VIEW THE CHARMS OF THE JUNGFRAU

We had learned on our arrival that nearly everyone had left Interlaken about the fifteenth of the month, disgusted with the continued wet weather, that the Grimsel pass over which we proposed to go on our way into Italy had been closed by the snow and that diligence traffic over this pass always closes on September 15. But such delightful weather had prevailed during and several days prior to our arrival that we were informed if we would wait a day or two very likely the pass would be open again and we could cross it in a carriage from Meiringen.

Therefore, on September 29, when word came that the pass was again clear we shipped our trunks to Milan by the petite vitesse and started along the shore of Lake Brienz for the town of Brienz at the further end of the lake, less than twenty kilometers away. Interlaken, in fact, gets its name from its position between the lake of Thun and the lake of Brienz. The road from Interlaken to Brienz was excellent but the scenery was hardly as fine as that between Thun and Interlaken. Arriving at Brienz we found that we could get a one-horse carriage to take us across the Grimsel for forty-five francs, but we thought we might as well ride along the fifteen kilometres that separated us from Meiringen, as a carriage from there would be cheaper, and besides we hadn't had riding enough for the day.

We arrived at this point and found the Hotel Brunig quite a resort for American and English

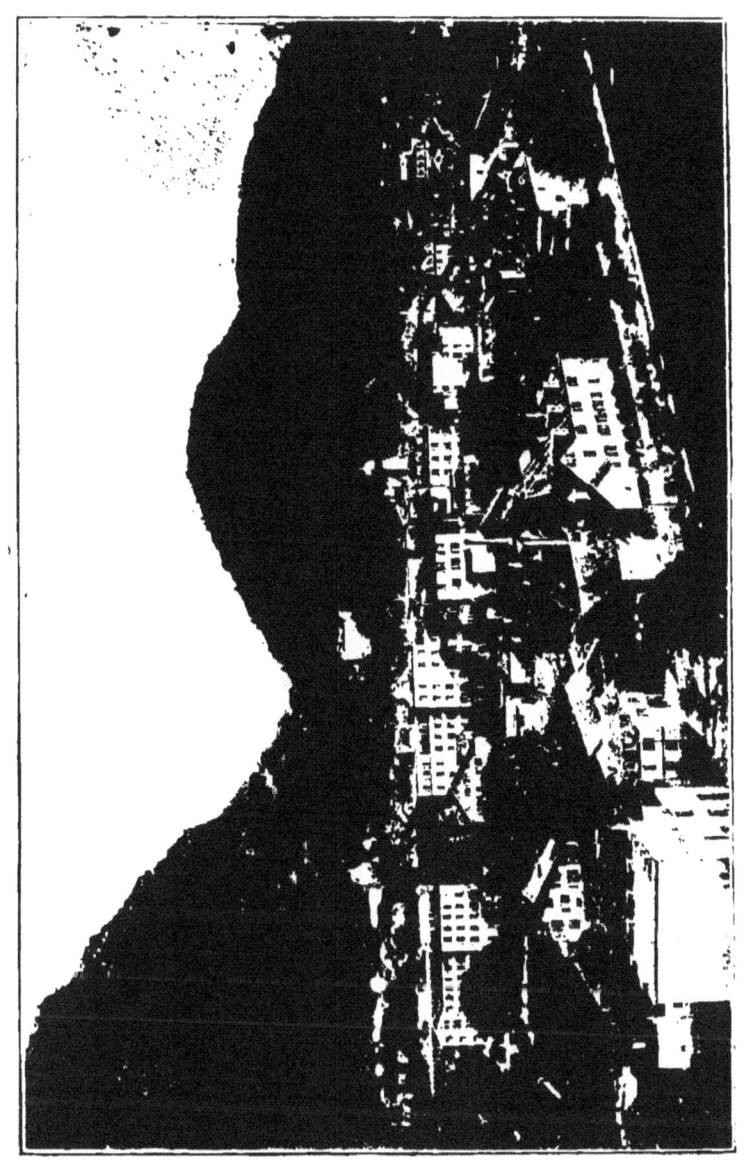

VIEW OF INTERLAKEN WITH THE JUNGFRAU IN THE DISTANCE.

people, about a dozen of whom still lingered on although the season was over. Many of the ladies came to table d'hote dinner in more or less of evening dress, but that didn't bother Lou, for she was quite at home in her short skirt and said she knew all the rest of them were envying her. As a matter of fact, judging from the conversation at the table, every member of that little company bicycled, from grandpa. who sat at its head, to the youngest child, a pretty little English girl about ten years old. Prices here were about the same as elsewhere, Joe and Lou paying only four francs for their room. The dinner though, was three francs for each person, without wine. However, we got a bottle of excellent Beaujolais for three francs.

That night we made an arrangement with a man who owned a one-horse carriage to take us up the Grimsel pass the next day for thirty-five francs. He would have taken two persons for thirty. It was arranged that we should start at 8:30 the next morning. When we came down we found the bicycles artistically attached to the back of the carriage by ropes and supported by boards. They were so arranged that there was little or no strain on them. The carriage was one of the landau pattern. After a cup of coffee we started on our long journey up the pass. The distance, all told, was about thirty kilometers and the horse could only average about four kilometers an hour. We were to breakfast at Handegg, where we were due about noon. I think that if I were doing it over again, and particularly if there were no ladies in the party, I would advise keeping on with the bicycles as far as Handegg, as part of the road to that point is rideable and one could make much better than four kilometers an hour up to that point. After breakfasting at Handegg, where we submitted to some mild extortion owing to the lack of competition, we set out again for the top of the pass. The trip through one of these passes is always wonderful and beautiful, and the journey through the Grimsel was extremely picturesque, the falls at Handegg being especially noticeable.

When we arrived at the top of the pass our driver who spoke neither English nor French, drew up his horse and, having received his money, began unfastening the bicycles. Then, with one sweep of his hand toward the left and indicating a mass of white snow and ice he said, "Rhona glacier;" then, pointing toward the right, he pronounced the words "Munster—Brigue." With that he was gone.

We now found ourselves in a rather peculiar position. It was nearly five o'clock and night was not far off. We were so high on the mountain top that the clouds were settling about us and it began to rain; before us lay that terribly steep zig-zag path down the mountain, covered here and there by sharp-pointed broken stones with which the road laborers had filled in mud holes, and elsewhere, by larger bits of rock, which, freed from their position by the melting snow, had rolled from the crags above.

This was the sort of roadway which confronted us, and to its right lay a precipice with an awful descent of hundreds of feet to the rocks below, with nothing between us and its edge save a number of stone posts about two feet high at intervals of thirty feet. It was a hard road for any man to undertake, let alone a woman, but Lou wouldn't hear of walking, so we all looked to see that our brakes were in good condition and warned Lou under no circumstances to let her wheel get beyond her control; if she found it was doing so to put on her brake hard and back pedal with all her might and then, if she still felt any doubt as to her ability to stop her machine, to promptly fall off before it had a chance to run away with her. Having taken these precautions we set out, not without misgivings but with a feeling that something must be done. After the first two kilometers we were out of the rain but the road grew no better. Yet every time that Joe and I, who were in advance, called back to Lou she replied that she was all right.

At the bottom of the mountain, and in fact during the last part of the descent, the road was not too steep for comfortable riding, but as it was already growing dark and as Brigue was still fifty kilometers away we had to give up all idea, of course, of getting there that night. but we did manage to make Munster, though we rode the last three kilometers in a heavy shower which had come up suddenly. It was quite dark when we reached this town and we now found ourselves among people who could speak practically nothing but German.

At the Hotel de la Croix d'Or et Poste, a hotel of unusual excellence for so small a place, we found, however, a young woman who spoke French quite well. We had a fire built in the parlor for us, and a couple of hot drinks and a good dinner made us all feel better. The prices were about the same as usual, only the rooms being cheaper. I was charged two francs for my room, while Joe paid three. The weather being fair the next morning we rode on to Fiesch, a little more than twenty kilometers from Munster. Here we breakfasted at the Hotel du Glacier et Poste. The check for the three of us amounted only to eight francs, including wine, coffee and cognac. The road from here to Brigue was still down hill and we made perhaps the fastest time on the trip in spite of the fact that several drivers of diligences made frantic attempts to run over us or force us off the road. Throughout Switzerland cyclists will notice this desire to kill cyclists which every diligence driver seems to nourish within his breast.

At Brigue, after making our usual reconnoitres, we finally went to the Hotel D'Angleterre, where we found the prices ranged a little higher than customary but here again our touring club card did us good service, securing for Joe and Lou the best room in the house for four francs, while I had a much smaller apartment and paid the same price. The dinners here were 3 francs 50 centimes, without wine, but wine was included with ours as a special concession.

We found that to get across the Simplon pass, or, that is, to be taken up to the Hospice, would cost with a one-horse carriage twenty francs. But as we thought we would be more comfortable with two horses, and as that cost only ten francs more, we made this arrangement.

The ride up the Simplon was quite as beautiful as that across the Grimsel, and this time, when our driver left us at l'Hospice, the sun was shining. This building was erected by the great Napoleon for the care of his soldiers during his first descent on Italy and is now occupied as a monastery. I had heard much of the hospitality of its inmates, but we searched it from top to bottom without being able to bring to light a single monk, much to Lou's disappointment.

The descent from l'Hospice is much less difficult to negotiate than on the Grimsel—from the effects of which, by the way, we were still suffering, our legs being stiff from back pedaling, as if we had taken a long ride for the first time in the season. Our hands, too, were stiff and cramped from where we had used the brake.

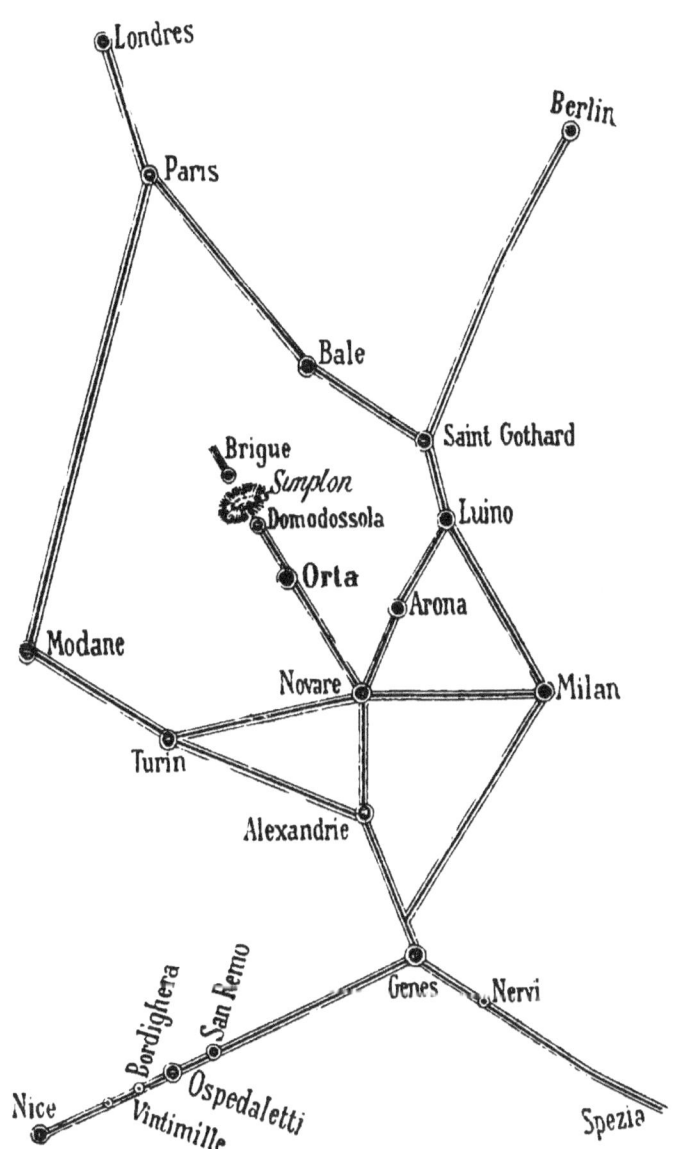

FROM BRIGUE TO MILAN, GENOA AND NICE.

From l'Hospice we had a delightful ride down to the town of Simplon, where we got an excellent breakfast at the Hotel de la Poste which, in spite of its unpretentious appearance, is well kept.

Soon after leaving Simplon we began to realize that Consul Ridgley was right in speaking of this route in the terms of highest praise. If there is any more beautiful bicycle trip it isn't to be found in the same sort of country. One might prefer a ride through miles of orange groves, or perhaps one's taste might run to the fragrant paths of a pine forest, or even the carefully kept cycle paths of the Bois du Boulogne, but for a trip, or rather a coast on a bicycle, alongside of rushing mountain streams in a narrow gorge where the rugged splendor of the surrounding scenery almost awes you, one might search the world over and find nothing to equal that coast from the Simplon across the Italian frontier to Domo d'Ossola.

CHAPTER XI.

First Impressions of Italy.

LL this route from the Simplon down is in the nature of one long coast and only two things interfered with our making twenty-five kilometers an hour. 'ne was the fact that in places where the sun's rays had been unable to reach there was more or less mud, and the other was Lou's tendency to keep us dismounting about every fifteen minutes while she had a chance to admire at her leisure some peculiarly striking bit of nature's handiwork. About half way between Simplon and Domo d'Ossola we crossed the frontier at a small place named Gordo. We could tell pretty surely when we were nearing the frontier by the sentry boxes with solitary sentinels which we remarked here and there before reaching Gordo itself. At the custom office we were politely received by an officer in uniform, who took our cards to a clerk at a desk inside. The cards were scrutinized carefully enough, but little care was taken in comparing the numbers and names on the cards with those on

the machines and as all our wheels were somewhat spattered with mud I have my doubts whether the custom house officials saw tne artistic 133 which Joe had so carefully cut in Lou's machine. Anyway we complied with all the formalities and on the payment of twenty-four cents each we got our receipts of entry and went on our way rejoicing. On our receipts the name of the town was stamped Gondo but all the maps give it Gordo.

It was nearly six o'clock when we entered the pretty town of Domo d'Ossola. Our first attempt at a hotel did not prove a success. The house was attractive in exterior appearance but as the waiters, the chambermaids, the porters, the stable boys, the cooks, together with the proprietor, his wife and four daughters all gathered around us at once and gibbered away in Italian we concluded it was no place for us and fled incontinently, even leaving the refreshments which we had ordered untasted on the table. Further along, in the center of the town, we found a less pretentious hotel known as the Albergo Manini, the proprietor of which had only two waiters and the good sense to speak French. Here Joe and Lou got very good rooms for three francs, while I didn't fare at all badly and only paid two. Among the changes that we began to remark was that the rooms no longer had two beds. In fact, no room of average size would have the space for two ordinary Italian beds. I hardly dare to say how large they are, but think I'm safe in stating that they are larger than billiard tables, and not so large as lawn tennis courts. To get as near as possible the exact dimensions I should say they ran from seven to ten feet wide. Among the other odd things that we noticed immediately after our advent in Italy was a custom, altogether too common, of serving the soup after the fish, and cold meats after the entrees and roasts had been eaten. Lou said it would not surprise her a bit to get her oysters after her ice cream if that sort of thing kept on.

We also noticed that when an Italian wanted to light his cigar after dinner the waiter would bring him a lighted candle to which an iron support was attached by a ring sliding up and down the candle itself. On this support the smoker would lay his cigar—generally about eight inches in length—with its end in the flame and let it burn away there for about five minutes before he began to puff on it. Lou said that she thought fried cigars must be just as bad as boiled milk. We were also rather disappointed in the Italian grape. We had always supposed that if you were going to get good grapes anywhere it would be in Italy, but so far as we could see they were very little better than can be had in the south of France. The Italians have one sensible custom, though, about serving grapes. They never bring a bunch of grapes to the table without giving you a large bowl to wash them in.

So attractive did we find Domo d'Ossola that we spent two nights there. Wheeling in the neighborhood was excellent and the table at the hotel very good. The dinners at the Albergo Manini were three francs with wine, a very fair red wine of the country. On October 4 we started out on our journey toward Milan, with a letter of recommendation from the proprietor of the hotel to his father, who kept a hotel at Orta.

We had planned to breakfast at Omegna, about half way to Orta, which was some forty kilometers from Domo d'Ossola, but when we got as far as Omegna we breakfasted so late that we decided to spend the night there, particularly as the sky looked overcast and Lou, who had had her hair curled before leaving Domo d'Ossola, declared that she didn't want to take the chance of another wetting. At Omegna we went to the Albergo Croce Bianca. Here the price of rooms dropped for Joe and Lou to three francs, or I should say three lire, which is equivalent to about the same thing, though really a little bit less. I paid two lire. The dinners were three lire each. The next day we spent roaming around the country and in the afternoon rode to Orta at the foot of a beautiful little lake of that name. Here we found the Hotel du Lion d'Or, charmingly situated and the prices as usual. We should have liked to linger there longer but we felt that we'd never get to Milan if we kept on spending two or three days at each place that we found particularly attractive.

The night of October 6 found us riding into Arona, a town of about four thousand inhabitants at the southern extremity of Lake Maggiore. After looking the hotels over we concluded that none of them amounted to much and finally settled at the "Albergo Ristorante Ruffoni," Gia' Falcone. This hotel had an excellent view of the lake and, though of decidedly modest pretentions, proved to be perfectly comfortable. Here again Joe only paid three lire while I escaped for two. We had planned to stay several days at Arona in order to make a tour of the lake on one of the lake steamers which cruise from point to point on either side of this beautiful sheet of water. As we were riding around Arona, the afternoon of our arrival, Lou noticed the sign of a bath establishment and after we had left our things at the hotel she announced that she was going back to get a good hot bath. She was gone about fifteen minutes and returned looking disgusted.

"What's the matter?" said Joe.

"Would you believe it," said Lou, "that old woman who runs that bath establishment said that if I wanted to take a hot bath I must let her know the day before so that she could get the fires lighted to heat the water?"

"How do you know she said that?" asked Joe.

"Oh, she didn't speak such bad French," said

Lou, "and she seemed quite surprised that I should find anything unusual in being obliged to give twenty-four hours' notice of my intention to take a bath."

Next day we took a steamer and went up the lake as far as Isola Bella, where there is a most interesting palace belonging to one of the oldest families of the Italian nobility. This trip on the Lake Maggiore is something that no one who passes through Arona, or is even as near as Milan, should miss.

After another day's tour in the neighborhood, both by boat and wheel, we set out for Milan by the way of Gallarate and Legnano. This made a ride of sixty-five kilometers.

En route, however, we stopped at a place called Lorenzo to get breakfast and there Lou got it into her head that her hind tire wasn't blown up tight enough to suit her ideas of rigidity. Joe and I managed to pump it up for her but in some way or another something happened to the valve and our united ingenuity could not make the air stay in that blessed tire. So there we were, more than twenty kilometers from Milan with Lou's wheel in an unrideable condition. No one about the place spoke anything but Italian, but Joe got out his pocket dictionary and carried on a long conversation with one Italian more intelligent than the rest, who made us understand that in about an hour a steam tramway would pass the door which would take us right into the city, bicycles and all, for twenty cents apiece. Then we felt better and had breakfast. By the way, if you are afflicted by a large appetite and a small pocketbook, go to Lorenzo, Italy, and become a boarder at the Ristorante Dell 'Angelo. The breakfast for us three cost fifty-nine cents, which was divided up in this way: Wine eight cents, bread four cents, an enormous plate of fried potatoes sixteen cents, milk and butter for Lou twelve cents, a large plate of chops s.xteen cents, one pony of kummel three cents. This certainly was cheap enough and we had more than we wanted.

Naturally we were all somewhat disappointed in not being able to ride into Milan, but felt that we were very fortunate to have the tramway so near at hand, and, although, when we were once on board we were carried along pretty fast, we got a fair view of the country, which wasn't nearly as interesting to us as the people. On leaving the car the first thing we did was to look up a repairer of bicycles and he soon had Lou's machine in running order. We were surprised on riding through Milan at the attention which Lou attracted. We expected this sort of thing in the country and smaller towns, but in a city like Milan, of more than 300,000 inhabitants, we hadn't supposed she would attract any more attention than sne would in New York. Still it was a fact, and we couldn't help noticing it, that people stopped in the streets, turned around and stared after her.

Later on we learned that ladies ride comparatively little in Milan and then confine their wheeling to the park, seldom appearing in the city itself.

It is more difficult to find the right kind of lodgings in a large city than in the smaller towns that one rides through when touring. After many disappointments in the way of quarters which proved unsuitable either because they were too dear or too cheap, more by good luck than anything else we stumbled upon the Hotel St. Michel and Bernerhof, situated right in the heart of the city. If the street which it is in has any name I never knew it, and the proprietor doesn't put it on his bill heads. It stands in the first street back of the cathedral, or the first street to the right off the Corso Victor Emanuel. Any cabman in Milan knows the Hotel St. Michel, as it is commonly called.

We had planned to stay some time in Milan, and finding that we could have our meals at any hour that suited us we agreed to pay so much a day for our meals with board. We wouldn't have thought of doing this if we had not had our own table in the restaurant and ordered just what we liked, as if we were living on the a la carte principle. We were at the hotel two weeks on this plan and found it very satisfactory, the only trouble being that there was a great deal too much of everything. Only the fires in our rooms were extra. The price we paid for all this, with wine included, was seven francs a day, each. It is useless for me to try to describe here the beauties of Milan. Baedeker will tell you all about it. All I can say is that it rained nearly all the time during those two weeks, and yet we were not bored. The theatre, the opera and the concert hall in Milan are within the financial reach of all and cabs can be had for thirty cents for the first hour, and twenty cents for all hours afterward. Milan is a wretched place to bicycle in, however, as the streets are narrow and choked up with traffic.

It was not till October 18 that the weather was pleasant enough to warrant our starting on our ride to Venice. On the afternoon of that day we started out at 3 o'clock in the afternoon and rode to Lodi, some thirty-one kilometers from Milan. We got there while it was still light and went to the Albergo Ristorante Vignola, where we got rooms for seven francs, four of which fell to Joe's share. The hotel is on the main square of the town, known as the Piazza Maggiore, and nearly opposite was the restaurant Vedova, where we all dined comfortably for a dollar. In the morning Lou was much interested in a market which was being held in the square, attended by peasants from all the country around. We got under way about 11 o'clock, and riding across the bridge made famous by the charge of the French troops, led by the great Napoleon himself, we cycled sixteen kilometers to Crema, where we breakfasted at the Albergo Ponte di Rialto. By this time we had learned Italian enough to know that vino was wine, pane was bread, uova fritta was fried eggs and uva was grapes. We had also grasped the fact that caffe was coffee and latte meant milk. In fact, Lou said she knew lots more things, and I guess she did by the confidence with which she kept saying to the peasants along the route, "quella strada andare to the next old place?"

After having paid the enormous sum of eighty cents for breakfast we started out again by the way of Romanengo, Soncino Pompiano and Torbole, and quite early in the afternoon had finished the thirty-three kilometers which lay between us and Brescia where we were to pass the night.

CHAPTER XII.

Nearing Venice.

I HAD no difficulty in finding a good hotel at Brescia as there were several all near together. Our choice was the Albergo dell 'Orologio, which was on the main square in the centre of the town. The young man in charge spoke French very well, and the price of a double room was only three francs. In the restaurant one is well served, a la carte, at the low prices prevailing in Italy. Brescia is pleasantly situated on a hill and commands a magnificent view and there are many things of interest to be seen there, besides the inevitable cathedral. In fact, we did not stay at Brescia as long as we should have liked to, for the next day was fair and we were anxious to push on to Verona, which was just sixty-six kilometers further on our way to Venice. We breakfasted at Lonato, a town of between 6,000 and 7,000 inhabitants, twenty-three kilometers from Brescia. The road to Verona we found excellent, although the weather was uncomfort-

ably warm, in spite of the fact that it was almost the end of October.

Among the other things which the cyclist notices in this part of Lombardy are the rows after rows of high hedges which line the road on either side and shut out, most of the time, whatever scenery there may be. But, as a rule, this country is flat and rather uninteresting. I should judge that the same thing is true of nearly all of Lombardy. Ordinarily, in cycling, one has a constant change of view and the road twists about bringing with each turn some change of scene, but this isn't the case on the road from Milan to Venice, where, for mile after mile one sees before him a great stretch of road without a single turn or deviation, which makes the way seem much longer. In fact, Lou said she'd rather climb a hill or put up with most any kind of wheeling if they would only give her a little variety.

As you wheel along, too, you can't help being struck with the fact that Italy must be the bargain counter of the world for statuary. Every estate along the road, whether the house thereon be a mansion or a modest cottage, is sure to have the statue of some well-known mythological character in life size on either gate post, and the walls enclosing the grounds are invariably decorated with the busts of those whose names have come down to us from the days of antiquity. And scattered about the grounds themselves are more statues, many of which, owing to their exposure to the weather, look more or less the worse for wear. In these cases Venus de Milo no longer has a corner on being the only statue without arms. Armless Apollos and legless Venuses, not to mention Jupiters minus an ear, are frequently seen, while many of the marble counterfeit presentments of Bacchus make that giddy young god look as if he had been out all night and had run into the club of a New York policeman.

However, all these things are amusing and Lou rather enjoyed the sensation she caused when we dashed through the small Italian hamlets and villages, where men and women ran out into the streets in a frantic endeavor to get a glimpse of the spirit from a foreign land who flew through their country on wheels. Still it is only fair to say that the Italians were only animated by sheer curiosity and that their attentions were never otherwise than respectful, if we except one case in Milan, where an irresponsible small boy threw a stick at Lou's wheel which broke the mud-guard. Joe would have liked to administer a good American spanking to this young son of Italy, but he fled like the wind and was soon lost in a crowd of his fellows.

From Lonato our way lay through Rivoltella, Peschiera to Castelnuovo di Ver. The last mentioned place is only eighteen kilometers from Verona, where we arrived just at dark. As it was raining at the time, we went to the first hotel we could find, which happened to be the Alla Gabbia, which is on the Piazza Erbe. This hotel was not as cheerful as it might have been, but still we were not uncomfortable there. A room for two persons cost four lire, and all the prices were quite as reasonable as those I have already mentioned.

We did not see Verona under the pleasantest circumstances and yet we enjoyed it thoroughly, although it rained almost incessantly while we were there. Really Verona is one of the most interesting cities of Italy, if not of all Europe. It is a perfect symposium of Roman antiquities and of cathedrals decorated by the greatest masters known to Italian art. Its amphitheatre is believed to have been constructed in the years 68 and 69 A. D., and almost all of its celebrities of past ages can boast of having been dead longer than similar celebrities almost anywhere else in Italy. Naturally we visited all the cathedrals most worthy of our attention, besides making an inspection of the fortifications of the city, which are most complete and interesting.

I think what Lou enjoyed most was our call at the alleged tomb of Romeo and Juliet. I say tomb, although what we saw was only a small part of it. In appearance it resembled a great stone bathtub, which was more than half filled with the visiting cards which had been left there by sympathetic callers from all parts of the world. Lou followed the example of her predecessors and dropped a dainty little card, and, I suspect, a tear where so many similar cards and possibly tears had been dropped before. We were told afterwards that there are really no authentic proofs that what is pointed out to the visitors at Verona as part of the tomb of Romeo and Juliet is really what it is supposed to be, but Lou would never listen to the story for an instant. She declares she is sure that that stone bathtub is the real thing for she felt the presence of the unfortunate lovers as she stood beside it. One thing that troubled Lou in Verona, as elsewhere in Italy, was the idea that Garibaldi, who had been dead only such a short time, should have so many more statues than lots of other distinguished Italians who died centuries before he was born.

On the morning of the third day, as it was still raining, we made up our minds that if it hadn't cleared up by afternoon we would go by rail to Vicenza, which was fifty kilometers further along on our road to Venice. Therefore, as the weather was unchanged in the afternoon, we took a train about four o'clock for Vicenza. But as we rode over this same route on our wheels on our way back from Venice, I am prepared to say that the wheeling between the two cities is not at all bad.

On arriving at Vicenza we left our bicycles at the station, having unstrapped what baggage we carried on them. Then, for the first time and the last while on a wheeling tour in Europe, we entered one of the hotel omnibuses which was waiting at the station. A little later we had a chance to see for ourselves at what a disadvantage any one is who makes his entry into an Italian hotel under these circumstances.

The particular omnibus which we got into belonged to the Hotel Roma, which is some distance from the station. When the omnibus stopped we found ourselves in the courtyard of a hotel of considerable dimensions. The manager, who spoke French, said he had rooms for two persons as low as six francs. Lou elevated her eyebrows at this but said she would look at the quarters. Joe and I went up with her and were shown to a miserable little inside room with single bed. It was the worst thing in the way of rooms that we had seen since we left Paris. The waiter volunteered the information that they had something better for ten lire. There is no denying the fact that we were three pretty mad Americans when we got down stairs.

The manager was standing on a chair winding a clock, surrounded by four or five waiters, when we tackled him. Briefly, but in fervent language, we told him what we thought of him and his hotel and then before he had time to even get off his chair we each grabbed up our hand baggage and sailed out of the hotel. I don't think there was a more astonished hotel manager or a madder one in all Italy that night. A waiter followed us up the street trying to get a lira each from us for our fares in the omnibus to the hotel. We paid no attention to him. Having sought out the nearest cafe we had no difficulty in being directed to an excellent hotel near by where Joe got a splendid double rooom for three lire and the restaurant was not only good but the prices in the restaurant were even lower than some of those already cited.

We did little or no sight seeing in Vicenza, and though we breakfasted there we did not make a start till afternoon. It was Sunday and we attracted a good deal of attention when we made our appearance in the street. We arrived at Padua, thirty-two kilometers from Vicenza, so early in the afternoon that we thought we might as well keep on towards Venice, or rather Mestre. which is as far as one can go on one's wheel. At Mestre you take the boat or the train across the bridge to Venice. Mestre is only forty-two kilometers from Padua. We knew we couldn't reach Mestre that afternoon but thought we might arrive at Mira Vecchia, a town of nearly ten thousand inhabitants, where we could pass the night. That afternoon, however, for the first time we lost our way. We made the mistake of asking in our Nutt's dictionary Italian if we were on the right road to Venice. In each case we were assured that we were. The good people that we met had no intention of deceiving us but while we were always riding towards our destination we were entirely off the road to Mira Vecchia. When we discovered this fact it was already dark and the nearest town at which we could find accommodations for the night was called Mirano and was nearly ten kilometers away. There was nothing for it, however, but to make the ride in the dark. We had no lanterns, but managed to reach Mirano without accident between seven and eight o'clock. Here there was no question as to hotels. There was only one in the town. The main square of the town was lighted up and a brass band was playing in the center of it. Lou said she wondered how they knew we were coming. We were too glad to get anywhere to ask any questions about prices that night, but when we got our bill next morning we could hardly believe our eyes.

Joe and Lou had a room which was nearly big enough for a bowling alley, with the usual decorated ceiling and painted walls. The charge for this for both of them was thirty cents, or fifteen cents apiece, while my room, which wasn't quite so large, was twenty cents. Dinner for us three was eighty cents, and three pints of wine were marked down as eighteen cents. The Benedictines, cognacs, etc., as well as the small cups of coffee were all charged for at the rate of two cents each. We could hardly believe that there had not been some mistake until we had paid the bill and received our receipt. Then we came to the conclusion that this must have been the first time any Americans had ever stayed over night at Mirano. We were very careful not to spoil a good thing by expressing surprise or by giving over-extravagant tips. On inquiring in the morning where we were we found that we had only about ten kilometers to reach Mestre. We had to walk and push our machines, however, to get out of Mirano, as it was market day there and the streets were filled with peasants.

The road to Mestre proved all right, and on arriving there, instead of leaving our wheels in the town itself, we followed the horse car track and rode out to the end of the point of land from which a little passenger steamer starts for Venice. There we found a storage room, prepared especially for the keeping of bicycles, at a cost, if I remember rightly, of five or six cents a day. On arriving at Venice we had no idea where to go, so on leaving the steamer we hired a gondola by the hour and were propelled up and down the Grand canal looking for suitable quarters. Of course Venice is dearer than most places in Italy, but we succeeded in getting excellent quarters at the Hotel Beau-Rivage very reasonably. There a room cost Joe and Lou six francs a day, while I paid four. Cafe au lait with bread and butter, served in the room, cost twenty-five cents. At the Ristoratore Panada on the Calle Specchieri, Nos. 647 and 648, there is a restaurant which furnishes a remarkable variety of dishes and wines at prices which seem ridiculously cheap. If

NO BICYCLING IN THE PLACE ST. MARC

they ordered sensibly two persons could spend a dollar for dinner at this restaurant, without wine, but they would have to have a great appetite. Birds and fish of all varieties are specialties here and they have an excellent Italian champagne also, which is fairly dry, and costs only about sixty cents a bottle. At this moment I cannot be sure of the spelling of the name, but if you ask for a bottle of Cognegliano I am quite sure that you will get what I mean.

Your guide books will tell you more about Venice than I could possibly find room for here, so there is no use of my attempting to go into the beauties and charms of this peculiar city. In its way it is perhaps the most interesting city in Europe.

Naturally you can't bicycle in Venice and Lou regretted much that we hadn't sent at least one trunk on from Milan. Hers was the only short skirt we saw while there, and while one gets more or less used to being stared at, too much of that sort of thing becomes trying to the nerves. Lou didn't say much about it, but it was easy to see what she thought on the subject, for one day she stamped her foot in vexation and almost with tears in her eyes exclaimed:

"I wouldn't care so much if I was only sure these people knew I was cycling. What I'm afraid of is that some idiot will go and think that I am a new woman, or some awful thing like that."

A STREET WHERE ONE WOULD NEED AN AQUATIC BICYCLE.

However, as we spent most of our time out of doors in gondolas, the length of the skirt didn't make much difference after all except in crossing the Place St. Marc on our way to the restaurant or while out on shopping tours.

We spent six days in Venice, and on October 30 we returned to Mestre and set out on our return journey over the same route which we had taken on our way to Venice, with the exception that we rode back by the way of Mira Vecchia instead of going back by Mirano. At Verona the weather had grown so cold that we took the train back to Milan, where we spent another week at the Hotel St. Michel.

This time instead of taking pension, or board, we lived on the European plan. Joe and Lou got an excellent room with an electric light for five lire a day, while I did fairly well for two lire less. We breakfasted and dined at the hotel or outside, as we saw fit, and found that there was not much difference in expense between this plan and the one we had adopted before of paying seven francs a day, which covered everything.

At the end of the week as the weather grew no warmer, we determined to take the train to Genoa, and cycle along the Mediterranean from Genoa to Nice. Although we took the train, in the proper season one can cycle very easily from Milan to Genoa by the way of Pavia, Tortona Cassano Spinola, Ronco Scrivia and Busalla. The distance from Milan to Tortona is forty-six kilometers; from Tortona to Genoa it is seventy-five kilometers.

CHAPTER XIII.

On To Ventimiglia.

ON LEAVING MILAN we had sent our trunks on by the grande vitesse, so when we left the train on arriving at Genoa, we fastened our baggage as usual to our machines and started to ride through the city in quest of a hotel which would prove to our liking. We hadn't ridden fifty yards, however, before a very tall man of sombre mien, wearing a tall hat and a long, single-breasted coat, buttoned up high about the neck, and reaching nearly to his ankles, stepped into the middle of the narrow street, and holding before him a kind of mace he carried, bade us politely enough to dismount.

This individual was one of those peculiarly garbed policemen whom one sees in the large cities of Italy. The officer spoke only a few words of French, but he made us understand that it is forbidden to ride the wheel in Genoa. Later on, when we inquired why, we were told that nearly all the traffic in the city passes through the single main thoroughfare, which is badly paved and very narrow. Of course, we were surprised, but there was nothing else to do but accept the situation gracefully. We pushed our wheels before us to the Hotel des Etrangers, which is situated on the Rue Carioli, quite in the centre of Genoa. It is an excellent hotel, with electric lights and elevators and is heated throughout, but Lou thought nine lire was rather high for the room to which she and Joe were shown. The proprietor was a most agreeable man and admitted very frankly that the hotels in general in Genoa were dearer than anywhere else in Italy, and then added that since we were members of the French Touring Club he would make the price of the room six lire. I also had an excellent room for a lira less. The restaurant was a la carte and the cuisine very good, and for the first time in many days we were able to get a sirloin steak, which would have been a credit to any first-class American restaurant.

The next morning, as bicycles were tabooed, we took a carriage for a drive through the town. I think the carriage, which made a very good appearance, was forty cents an hour. We were more anxious to see the house where Columbus was born than anything else. Having seen that and the fortifications and other points of interest in the city, we went back to the hotel and had our bicycles taken to the sta-

YOU CAN'T CYCLE IN GENOA; COLUMBUS DIDN'T.

tion. We did this because everyone agreed that the first sixteen kilometers from Genoa, or as far as Voltri on our way to Nice, was an abominable route for wheelmen. Therefore, we took the train which left Genoa about two o'clock, for Voltri. The train ran along close to the shore of the Mediterranean, and whenever it stopped, for any reason, the passengers amused themselves by throwing coppers out of the windows for the children of the fishermen who swarmed the beach, to scramble for.

In about half an hour we were at Voltri and had mounted our wheels and begun our ride to Nice. The distance from Nice to Genoa is in the neighborhood of 175 kilometers. That afternoon we rode a little more than thirty kilometers to Savona, a town of about 30,000 inhabitants where we found very good accommodations and courteous treatment at the Hotel Roma. Our rooms here were four and five lire, respectively, and the prices at the restaurant were about the same as usual.

On the morning of November 8 the weather was simply perfect. The air was warm and balmy without being too hot, though in riding in the middle of the day we suffered a little from the heat, being clad too warmly. The road from Savona to Spotorno was simply a bicycling dream. On our left lay the beach washed by the blue waters of the Mediterranean. On our right rose great hills that sheltered us completely from the cold winds of the north. The scenery, people, and their habitations were all picturesque, and everything about us was full of interest. The road itself was good, and, taken altogether, I don't think that one could bicycle anywhere under more perfect conditions than along this route from Genoa to Nice. But, alas! for us, it was not to be, and as we bowled along, all of us in the highest spirits, Lou declared without the slightest idea that her prediction was so soon to come true, that the only fear that she had was that it was just too lovely to last. At Spotorno, we dismounted from our wheels, and leaning them up against the side of the road, went down on the beach to see a score of fishermen, and women, for that matter, draw in a great net which had been set over night. The net was of enormous proportions, and stretched out to sea for a distance of about a hundred yards, and took at least a quarter of an hour to be drawn in. At last when the final meshes were drawn upon the beach, it was seen that the catch was a poor one, as there were not more than a bushel basket full of small fish to reward so many fishers for their labor.

Spotorno was perhaps the prettiest village we saw on our ride along the Mediterranean. It is delightfully situated at the base of two great hills, which slope down towards it gradually, leaving it charmingly land-locked on all sides from which a blast of cold air might possibly come. The houses, and the gardens about them, are attractive, and the people kind and hospitable. Along the beach were scores of fishing boats, showing that the fishing thereabouts must be good. Undoubtedly one could live in Spotorno, or in fact, in any of these Italian villages for about seventy-five cents a day, and be regarded as a millionaire. As we contemplated the natural beauties of the place, we couldn't help thinking how any one who wanted to withdraw from the noise and bustle of the world, and put aside the cares of life temporarily, might do well to resort to some such sequestered nook. Here one could find perfect rest and quiet. Surrounded by plenty of books, one would have no lack of time to read. Here, too, a knowledge of the Italian language could be acquired and no better place could be imagined for the finishing of some literary effort. For sport, one would have to depend on fishing, swimming, bicycling and tennis. Besides one could wheel to Monte Carlo and Nice by passing only one night somewhere on the road, or, in fact, a good wheelman could make the trip in one day.

Two or three kilometers beyond Spotorno we had other things to occupy our thoughts, for in going through the town of Noli, Joe's hind tire picked up a tack or nail which had doubtless worked loose from the wooden shoe of some Italian peasant. It made a good sized hole, and it was soon evident that Joe could do no more riding until that tire was repaired. It was a single tube American tire, but when we tried to repair it we could make no headway, as we could not force the mushroom-shaped bit of rubber into the hole, and found, moreover, that our glue had dried up. Fortunately, however, although it was Sunday, we found that a train was due in about half an hour, which would take us on to Finalmarina, nine kilometers further on, where there was a man who repaired bicycles. At this town we found the bicycle repair shop to be in charge of Emanuel Maggi, who, in reply to our dictionary Italian, looked confident and assured us that he could repair the tire easily, though he had never seen one like it before. Later on in the afternoon he was just as confident as ever, but hadn't made any headway with the tire or with his work. Finally, he said it would be necessary for us to stay all night.

Lou didn't like this idea, and said she'd bet he would charge us for sitting up all night with a sick tire. By noon the next day he sent word to the hotel that he'd finished his work and we all got ready to go down to the shop to congratulate him.

Finalmarina's hotel is not such a bad one. It is in the centre of the town, and is known as the Grande Hotel Garibaldi. We had ordered a la carte, and found things reasonable, and now on getting word from the bicycle man that he was ready for us, we called for our bill and found that the rooms were only marked at two and three lire respectively.

At the bicycle shop we found an admiring crowd gathered, who were watching Signor Maggi careering around the Square on Joe's wheel, just to show his countrymen that he could repair anything in the tire line, if it did come from America. That tire certainly did stand up, but what he had done to it we shall never know, even in the light of subsequent events.

The tire had been a new one when we left Milan. It now looked as if it had been ridden across the Rocky Mountains. Over the point where the nail had entered he had glued on several layers of rubber, and over this he had wound several yards of white cloth, all of which was fastened down with a piece of red flannel. Signor Maggi explained that if the tire didn't have a relapse after being ridden two or three hours we could remove these outside bandages. He then charged us eight lire for his work and said good morning and prepared to receive the congratulations of his friends.

The appearance of Joe's tire certainly wasn't calculated to inspire confidence in any one, but we mounted and started on all the same. For something more than fifteen kilometers we rode along all right, the wheeling and the scenery being almost equal to that which I have already described. As we were approaching Albenga, however, Lou and I, who were riding on ahead to warn Joe of any obstructions in the path, which might prove fatal to his already demoralized tire, heard him behind using language. We rode back and found the tire gone, this time for good and all we feared. Signor Maggi, after making his repairs, had put the tire back on the wooden rim with little or no glue. As a consequence the friction had cut the rubber badly about the valve. It was only about three kilometers to Albenga, so Joe climbed on a passing omnibus with his wheel, while Lou and I rode.

At Albenga we took luncheon at the Hotel Vittorrio, while a local bicycle professor tried to see what he could do with Joe's tire. He, too, thought he could fix it, but being a more honest man than Signor Maggi, frankly confessed his inability to do so, when we returned to the shop after luncheon.

THE CYCLIST'S ENEMY.

CHAPTER XIV.

Forced to Forsake Our Wheels.

HILE AT THE HOTEL we had engaged in conversation with an Italian army officer who spoke French, who told us that we would certainly be able to have the necessary repairs made at Oneglia, a city of 7,000 inhabitants, about forty kilometers further along on our journey.

An hour later we were in a train on our way to Oneglia. As we rode on the cars we could see enough of the route along which we would have ridden on our bicycles, but for Joe's accident, to make us all regret extremely that we were obliged to miss it. In fact, as far as we could judge, every bit of the way to Nice on the road which we had mapped out was as attractive as that part of it that we had already ridden. It was between four and five o'clock when we got to Oneglia, and as we were now nearing the French frontier, we found plenty of Italians ready to serve as interpreters for us in that language. As soon as we had stated our case, a consultation of all the bicycle professors of Oneglia was held, who, after a careful examination of the tire and conferring among themselves, gravely announced that the tire was beyond their aid. When we tried to buy a new tire they said they had none which could be mounted on a wooden rim, so we gave it up in despair and took the train that night at half-past seven for Nice.

Ventimiglia, the town on the frontier of France and Italy, which the railroad goes through, was only about forty kilometers away. This was the first time we had crossed the frontier with our bicycles on the train, but we didn't have the trouble we anticipated. On the presentation of our cards of identity and the slips given us at the time of the entries of the machines into Italy, we were passed through all right, although the official in charge said it would be unnecessary for him to take the time to write out a receipt to the effect that we had taken our machines out of the country. When we insisted, however, he complied with a rather bad grace and the remark that it wouldn't be his fault if we lost our train. He said no question would ever come up about the duties on our machines not having been paid, but we told him that we owed it to the Touring Club of France, which was responsible for us, to have our receipt in proper form.

On arriving in Nice, between ten and eleven

o'clock, we were all pretty tired, and went to the first hotel which we ran into on leaving the station, which happened to be the Hotel St. Louis. Still in Nice there is almost any number hotels at all prices, and if you don't care for hotel life, furnished lodgings can be had all over the city, which give very fair accommodations for from sixty francs a month up. The rooms which we had at the St. Louis were only up one flight, and were on the street. Five francs for Lou and Joe and four francs for me, with service and light included, was the price agreed upon. The morning after our arrival we found, to our consternation, that our trunks, which we had intrusted to Johnson & Son, in Milan, to be forwarded to us at Nice, had not yet arrived, although that was nearly a week ago. This was the more annoying, as we had agreed to pay more than five dollars in order to have them sent by the most rapid express. Joe had a brand new tire in his trunk, and was obliged to hire a wheel until its arrival. Lou, too, was annoyed, of course, at being obliged to go around in a short skirt, although that is so common at Nice that it attracts little or no attention.

This delay, however, led to our taking one useless trip. One afternoon we rode over to Monte Carlo, thinking to have a look at the Casino there, but were politely informed that we could not enter in bicycle costume. Lou said she didn't see why a man couldn't lose just as much money in a bicycle suit as he could in evening dress and that a short skirt might be an indication of a long pocketbook. This ride from Nice to Monte Carlo is a pretty hilly one, but is sufficiently picturesque to make it worth the while. It is less than twenty kilometers, anyway.

On the third day we got our trunks, at last, so Joe had his tire and Lou had her dresses, and everyone was happy.

I don't think that anything that I could write of our experiences in Nice could possibly add to that city's reputation as a popular winter resort. I can only say that we enjoyed ourselves there thoroughly and that it is a very pleasant city to bicycle in. I may add, too, that on a subsequent visit to Monte Carlo, in more conventional raiment, we looked in at the Casino and found that the bad luck which pursued us on the road attended us no longer. Joe won enough money playing roulette to buy more tires than he is ever likely to need in the rest of his natural life, while, if Lou puts her winnings into hats, she will be able to start a millinery store when she gets back to New York.

It had been our intention to return to Paris by the way of Marseilles, riding to that city from Nice on our wheels, but Joe received a cablegram which made it necessary for him to get home as soon as possible. For this reason we took the train direct from Nice to Paris.

CERCLE DES ÉTRANGERS DE MONACO

N° 1249

CARTE D'ADMISSION PERSONNELLE valable _____ délivrée

pour _____

à M _____

Monte Carlo, le 12 Novembre 1897

Le Commissaire Spécial,

Cette Carte doit être présentée pour l'entrée dans les salons et peut être retirée

YOUR PERMIT TO LOSE MONEY—OR WIN IT.

We left at ten-thirty in the evening and were in Paris the following day by six o'clock in the afternoon. Lou's last words were, as she stepped into the train for Havre, at the St. Lazare station:

"You may be sure that next summer you'll see me back in Europe for another tour, and in the meantime, I'm going to make Joe learn to repair his own tires."

Lou's speaking of summer tours recalls a little trip which we three took in June of 1897. On this occasion Joe was very much pressed for time, and we had only two weeks in which to ride. In that time, however, we rode in France, Belgium, Holland and even had a little run in Germany. On this tour we met with no accidents of any sort, and rode a thousand kilometers without any of us being obliged to do more than have our tires blown up now and then.

We left Paris about June 10th en route for Brussels, where the exposition was being held. As I have already said, in starting on a trip from Paris, one is apt to find the worst roads in the first day's ride from the city. For this reason, we decided to take the train to Laon, a little more than three hours' ride from Paris by rail. We left Paris from the Gare du Nord about noon. Laon is a town of about 14,000 inhabitants, and has a cathedral built in the thirteenth century, and an old tower and gate of the twelfth century. A beautiful view can also be had from the ramparts above the town.

We arrived at Laon so late in the afternoon that we decided not to stop to view the sights there, but to keep on instead to Vervins, a little more than twenty kilometers further on. You will have to take one or two hills on this route, but on the whole it isn't at all bad. At Vervins we went to the Hotel du Cheval Noir. This proved to be a very nice little hotel and we were soon well acquainted with our host, who seemed very much interested in us. Joe and Lou had an excellent room for two francs, while I paid the same for mine. The dinners were three francs each, with all the wine we could drink.

The next morning it was pretty hot, but we started out gaily for La Capelle, where we had planned to breakfast. Before we negotiated the twenty-five or thirty kilometers which lay between Vervins and this town, we realized that bicycling in the middle of a hot day was pretty serious business. However, on arriving at La Capelle, we went to the Hotel des Messageries, which had been recommended to us at Vervins. Here Madame Hergott and her very charming daughter showed us every attention, Miss Hergott even putting her own room at Lou's disposition. Half an hour's rest made us all feel better, and when the dejeuner a la fourchette was announced we were prepared to do it ample justice. We all enjoyed our stay at La Capelle extremely, and our hostess was very anxious to keep us over night, but we had determined to push on to Maubeuge, where we decided to spend the night. It was only about twenty-five kilometers to Maubeuge, which was a town of about nineteen thousand inhabitants. There we went to the Hotel du Grand Cerf. Here dinner, with wine, was, as usual, three francs, and we each paid two francs for our rooms. By the way of diversion that evening, we went to a cafe where there was a concert.

On leaving Maubeuge we found the roads rather heavy with mud, and we were obliged to depend almost altogether on the side paths and in some cases even these were not too rideable. It was also raining when we set out, but as Maubeuge is shut in in a sort of a valley, we rightly supposed that we would have clear weather after an hour's riding. After wheeling for about two hours we found ourselves on the Belgian frontier, where we were most politely received by two Belgian officers. We had left Paris in such a hurry that Joe and Lou hadn't had time to have their Touring Club cards properly made out and signed by the proper authority. However, the officials, as soon as tney had satisfied themselves that we were genuine tourists, allowed us to pass on without making any entry on their book at all, or without giving us any receipt of entry. Soon after crossing the frontier we found a path at the side of the road built exclusively for the use of cyclists. It was a cinder track, and, being wet, was a bit heavy, but was a welcome relief from the riding we had been having, and by this time ought to be in perfect condition.

At Mons, which is less than an hour's ride from the frontier, we stopped and had an excellent breakfast at one of the cafes, which are many and easily found there. Starting on our way again, the rain which had been threatening for some time, came down in earnest and at Soignie we took the train to Brussels.

Brussels is a town which has a reputation for cheap living. However that may be from the point of view of the native, or the foreigners who reside there, it is certain that in an exposition year the transient visitor will not be struck with this alleged characteristic of Belgium's capital. The hotels we tried were most of them expensive and didn't want to take you at all unless you took board as well as rooms. We finally secured very good rooms over Cordeman's restaurant, No. 2 Boulevard Anspach.

We liked this restaurant as well as any we found in Brussels, and it was very convenient for us living in that way. Joe paid four francs for his room and I paid the same for mine. Every citizen of the country who rides a bicycle has to carry a great white enamel plaque bearing a number on his machine, and the rules governing cyclists are quite strict. One officious young policeman stopped me because I had a gong or a "sonnette" on my machine instead of a bell or a "grelot." As I was a foreigner he didn't do anything more than give me a word of advice on the subject. Later on I asked an older policeman about this point, who told me that while the young officer might be technically right, he was evidently suffering from an attack of over-zeal. Joe also had an experience, being stopped by a policeman while coasting down a slight declivity near the exposition grounds. He was informed that bicyclists are not allowed to coast in Brussels. There were certain streets, too, which it is against the city ordinance for cyclists to ride through. Of course the foreign rider is not obliged to register his machine or carry a big plaque with a number, unless he means to make a prolonged stay there.

After several days in Brussels we started one afternoon for Antwerp, which is only two or three hours' ride from Brussels. Most of the way the road lies alongside of the canal, and much of it is shaded by great trees. Here, as almost everywhere else in Belgium and Holland, the road is level. This is one thing which makes cycling there easy and agreeable. Lou said that while she liked windmills and fields in the abstract, when one gets nothing but windmills and fields, with a few canals thrown in, in the way of scenery, it begins to grow a little monotonous

Something which we noticed on our way to Antwerp was that as we neared that city the bicyclists whom we met began to pass to our right, motioning us to take the left of the road. This seemed odd, as up to this point everybody had turned to the right. But the more we rode in Holland the less we were able to decide as to what the law of the road in that country is. We finally came to the conclusion that it was largely a matter of locality, and that in some parts of Holland you keep to the right, while in others you had to pass those whom you met on the left. We arrived in Antwerp on Sunday, and after riding through the city, went to the Grand Cafe Leopold. We ordered dinner on the terrace in front of the restaurant, and here we had an adventure which I will recount just as an instance of the strange experiences one meets with while touring.

CHAPTER XV.

Incidents of Travel.

THE dinner was ordered and after we had waited an unreasonably long time for the soup to be served, Joe called to the waiter, who at first paid no attention, and then, turning to us, said, insolently, "Don't disturb me when I'm busy, besides you're not an orchestra paid to make music for me."

The fellow's impudence was so astounding that at first we didn't know what to think. Then Joe went inside to interview the proprietor. The waiter followed him and continued his insolence in the hearing of his employer. In a moment the proprietor came out himself to take our order, and five minutes later the waiter, in his street clothes, with a little package in his hand, came up to our table and made an address in Belgian French something to this effect: "For three long years I have worked here, and now you see me discharged for you, a foreigner. But I am a man, and my hands are hard, and my arm is strong. Your hand is soft, your arm is weak. I go, but I will be revenged. You may sit here till long after midnight, but I will be on the watch from behind yonder tree."

Nobody made any reply to the man, thinking that he was simply drunk, and supposing that the proprietor would take him back the next day. An hour later, however, Lou looked up and exclaimed: "There's that dreadful man now." And sure enough there he was, on the opposite corner, talking to a woman and gesticulating and pointing to us in an excited manner.

A moment later he came up to the table again. This time with a stout stick, with its handle loaded with lead, under his arm. Again he made a little address, and then informed Joe that he was wanted at the police station. Still we paid no attention to the man, and he finally went away, only to return almost immediately, and this time with a policeman, who beckoned to Joe to leave the table and come out on the sidewalk. Instead of doing so, Joe sent for the proprietor, who said a word to the officer. The officer, proprietor and waiter then disappeared into the hotel. The next we saw of the man he came out of the side door alone with the policeman, who apparently was taking him off to the police station.

However, the incident rather spoiled the dinner and made Lou very nervous, and she dreamed all night that the waiter was at the front door waiting for us to come out in the morning in order to knock Joe's brains out with his loaded cane.

Lou's fears, however, were unfounded, as nobody was lying in wait for us when we mounted our wheels in front of the hotel in the morning. First we rode around Antwerp and took a look at some of the museums and two or three of the most interesting art galleries to be found there. For a continuance of the tour, we had planned that day to reach Eindhoven, which is more than fifty kilometers from Antwerp. On inquiry, however, we found that the first half of this distance was a combination of continuous ascent and bad roads. We therefore decided to take the train to Turnhout, which left us only between twenty and thirty kilometers to ride in order to reach Eindhoven. It may be well for me to state here that in Belgium and Holland you cannot have your bicycle carried on the train as cheaply or with the same facility as you can in France. In France, as I have said, you pay two cents, and on handing your wheel to the porter have no further trouble with it. In Belgium, on the contrary, you pay fifteen cents for your wheel and the employees of the railroad company are not obliged to handle it at all. Therefore, you are supposed to roll your wheel out on the railroad platform yourself and are often forced to put it in the baggage car with your own hand. Of course, this rule may have been changed since I was in Belgium, as the Touring Club of Belgium was trying when

I was there last summer to get some concession from the State in this respect. The troubles of the Belgium cyclists were generally attributed to the fact that the Minister whose department has charge of the railroads of that country is a crusty old bachelor who doesn't approve of cycling. Most of the Belgian railroads being operated by the State, his word is law about the matter.

However, we managed to get to Turnhout with our machines safe and sound, and then set out on our ride to Eindhoven, which we reached shortly before nightfall. The road between Turnhout and Eindhoven was very good as far as wheeling went, and in cycling through the small villages we did not encounter the same rough cobble stones with which the streets of similar places in France are paved. The main streets of the villages in Holland are also paved, but with peculiar elongated slabs of stone which are laid together in much the same manner as the strips of wood on a bowling alley. In the interior of Holland one finds few persons who speak either French or English, and one's ingenuity and the comprehensiveness of one's dictionary are taxed to the utmost.

On our arrival at Eindhoven we saw a dressmaker's sign in French and lost no time in calling on her to see whether she really was French or not. In this case she proved to be the real article, and after giving us such information as we desired, she directed us to the Hotel Posthuis, which was kept by a widow with three or four daughters. The hotel was a model of neatness and comfort, and the mother and the daughters spoke with considerable facility such French as they had acquired at boarding school. You must not expect to travel in Holland, or in Belgium, as cheaply as you can in France or Italy, or even in Switzerland for that matter. At Eindhoven the charge was three francs for each person's lodging, whether one or two persons occupied the same room. The dinners were two francs fifty centimes for each person without wine. In Holland wine is dear and not particularly good, but at Eindhoven we found for eight cents a large pony of cognac which far excelled anything we ever found elsewhere in Europe, even at one franc the thimbleful.

The following day Lou made her record ride of one hundred kilometers. She said afterwards if she'd known that we were making her ride so far she would have been too tired to have finished the day's journey. From Eindhoven we rode through a succession of fields and windmills to Weert, where we breakfasted at the Hotel de Roos. The name of the man who keeps the hotel is E. Coenegracht. How Mr. Coenegracht is going to get rich we couldn't quite understand. But then it was none of our business. Here was his bill for our breakfast: Eight beers, one glass of bitters, three breakfasts, three coffees with cheese, eighty-six cents. This would have been cheap even for

Italy, but we didn't run across this sort of thing often in Holland.

Leaving Weert, we passed through Maeseyck, and spent the night at Maastrick. We were now getting rather hurried, as we wanted to get back to Brussels in time to spend a day or two there.

The next morning we rode to Valkenberg, where there are really plenty of hills and scenery. This district is known as the local Switzerland, and Valkenberg is a very popular summer resort. We were now so near the frontier of Germany that we decided to cross it and ride to Aix la Chapelle, to take a look at Charlemagne's tomb and some of the bits of the cross on which the Saviour was crucified. Anyway, they said they were bits of the cross, and it cost two francs apiece to see them, so I guess they were. Neither in entering Germany nor in crossing the frontier again, two hours later, were we molested at all by the customs officials. Riding back from Germany we rode for about an hour in Holland, and on the Belgium frontier we had a little adventure.

At the custom house we showed our imperfectly prepared cards of identity to a subordinate official, who told us that we could proceed. Lou and I rode on, while Joe stopped to arrange something about his machine. Supposing he was following us, we rode on about eight kilometers before we decided to wait for him. When he did catch up with us he told us that he had had a great time with a higher official, who had come out and rebuked his subordinate for having allowed us to pass. He told Joe that he wasn't a Frenchman—no one could ever hear Joe's accent and think for an instant that he was—and said that the fact that we had ridden on showed that there was something irregular about us. With great difficulty Joe had persuaded the official to allow him to go on. The permission was accompanied by the information that he intended to wire custom officers at some point along our route to hold us up and examine all of our papers most carefully.

Lou said he needn't have taken all of that trouble, as the only thing irregular about Joe and me was our habits. As a matter of fact, we never heard of the matter again. That night we slept at Verviers, at the Hotel de l'Aigle Noir, 42 Place du Martyr. Here lodgings were 30 cents for each person, and the restaurant, where we dined a la carte, was very reasonable. The following morning we breakfasted at Pepinster and then rode on to Rochefort, where we visited the famous grottoes, which are well worth seeing, and attract people from all parts of Europe. Les Grottes de Han are said to be finer even than the grotto of Rochefort. They are near by, but we didn't have time to go there, and as the weather began to be bad, we took the train that afternoon for Brussels. While in Brussels we rode out to the scene of the

WHERE WELLINGTON SLEPT ON THE EVE OF
NAPOLEON'S WATERLOO.

battle of Waterloo, a trip which no one who visits Brussels should fail to take. The wheeling out and back was very good, and the round trip is only a matter of about thirty kilometers. A ride out to Aywaille and to the Bois de la Cambre are also well worth while.

After twenty-four hours in Brussels we had just time to ride back to Paris over the route by which we had come before the two weeks were up. It was in the following September that we set out on our ride to Venice, which has already been described.

CHAPTER XVI.

European Traveling as seen by Mr. Luce

R. ROBERT LUCE, of Boston, who has traveled much in Europe and who lectures on "Switzerland," "From Monte Carlo to Venice," "Rome," "The Bay of Naples," and other kindred subjects, has published a little book, entitled "Going Abroad?" which comprises much useful information for tourists generally, from which I cull the following extracts, with the permission of the author. Mr. Luce's book, which contains about 200 pages, covers nearly every branch of European travel and can be had by addressing Robert Luce, 68 Devonshire St., Boston, or through your newsdealer. The price of the book is 50 cents, paper, or $1 in cloth.

Mr. Luce makes a reference to an organization for women, which I have already mentioned as existing in Boston, and adds some comments of his own as to the conditions under which unprotected women travel abroad. On these subjects Mr. Luce says:

In the mere matter of travel Europe offers far more comfort and convenience than America to women journeying alone or in parties without men. They need never touch their luggage unless they choose. At hotels and railway stations they will always be more courteously treated than men—and that is saying a good deal. And the "unprotected female" needs no protection. English women think nothing of taking their vacations on the Continent, and a journey from New York to Los Angeles presents more terrors than one from London to Constantinople or Cairo.

To make foreign travel still easier, there exists an admirable organization called the Women's Rest Tour Association, which may be addressed at 264 Boylston Street, Boston. "Its object is to furnish women who wish to travel for purposes of rest and study with such practical advice and encouragement as shall enable them to do so independently, intelligently and economically. It is not designed for the convenience of women who organize or conduct large parties." And it may be added that it is in no way a money-making institution, there being neither salaries nor dividends for anybody in it. Mrs. Julia Ward Howe is the president, and other well-known New England women are on the board of officers. It publishes a handbook of travel, entitled "A Summer in England" (to which I would here give credit for some of the information hereafter given); issues yearly a revised list of accredited lodgings and pensions over all Europe, with details concerning prices and accommodations; publishes an occasional paper called The Pilgrim Scrip, devoted to travel and life abroad; exchanges introductions between members who desire company; lends money from its traveling fund (under careful supervision) to provide vacation trips for women greatly in need of rest and change; advises in regard to travel; lends from its library of Baedeker guide-books for the European trip; and in minor ways accomplishes its laudable purpose. The fee for the first year's membership is $2; annual fee thereafter, $1; life membership, $25. If but a small part of the wealthy American women who get enjoyment out of a trip abroad would, by becoming life members of this association, aid it in helping their less fortunate sisters to the same enjoyment, its sphere of usefulness could be greatly widened.

Speaking of the difficulty of securing berths on ocean steamers during the summer season, Mr. Luce says:

From November to April there is usually plenty of room, and travelers to whom crossing is an old story frequently take no more precautions than they would to secure a berth in a sleeping car for Chicago or St. Louis. In the winter, payment for a single berth usually secures a whole stateroom to yourself, and you have practically the pick of the boat. Sometimes on the smaller boats there will not be half a dozen first cabin passengers.

From the point of view of both economy and comfort, then, it is wiser if practicable to travel when the winter rates are in force. The fear of stormy weather doubtless deters many people from doing this, but the fact is that though the chances of severe storms are greater in winter than in summer, they are not enough greater to cut any figure with those who cross repeatedly. This matter of storms is largely one of luck.

Mr. Luce sizes up the climatic condition of various parts of Europe as follows:

Save in such sheltered spots as San Remo or Ventimiglia, the scenery of Italy is naturally at its worst in winter, for then the landscape is brown and bare. It is at its best in April and May, before the sun has begun to burn up things. June is a charming month at Venice, though some of its days are uncomfortably warm. In mid-summer the climate is much like that of the United States, frequently too hot for sight-seeing, yet with many comfortable periods. Few of the army of American tourists then go south of Florence, but European travelers, and especially Germans, think nothing of visiting Rome in July or August, and I have met people who declared they suffered not the slightest inconvenience at Naples in dog-days.

The notion that Rome must not be visited in summer on account of the malaria in the Campagna is no longer supported by those in a position to speak with authority. Of course it is dangerous to promenade after dark on the Campagna, just as it is in a Western river bottom, or anywhere else that malaria abounds, but tourists do not promenade on the Campagna after dark, nor do they drive across it after dark, as they often did before the time of railroads, when I suspect it was that Rome got its bad name as a summer resort. It does not yet deserve a good name, but it is no worse than our Southern States in the summer months, and if a tourist cannot well go south of Florence at any other time, there is little except the dread of perspiration to keep him from going in July or August.

The Italian summer is much like that of Virginia or Kentucky, comfortable enough, but less attractive than the spring.

Switzerland, for the passing tourist, is of course to be visited in summer, and in August rather than in June or July, if any mountain climbing is to be done, for while the snows are melting in early summer, the heights are the more dangerous. In September the air gets chilly and the shortening of the days is emphasized by the deep valleys. Many foreigners pass the winter about Lake Geneva, particularly at its eastern end, and there are a few winter resorts at high altitudes, almost wholly frequented by invalids for whose needs a peculiar climate is desirable; but to the ordinary traveler Switzerland in winter is dreary.

Germany's climate is much like that of New England and the Middle States, with plenty of snow and with skating a favorite amusement. Yet, though cold weather prevails, people who have passed winters in Germany and also in Italy, say they prefer Germany because the houses are warmly built and well provided with stoves.

Holland and Belgium are very cold in winter, and see few tourists at that season.

Athens has an equable climate, which in time is going to make it one of the most popular winter resorts on the Mediterranean. With the sea south of it, and hills rising to mountains behind, it has a situation midway that of an island and a continent. The spring and autumn there are charming; snow falls in winter only once or twice in years; fogs are rare. The summers are long, but the winds coming over the Aegean temper its heats.

Southern Spain is much like Southern Italy in winter. Water rarely freezes at Gibraltar. Oranges may be picked from the trees about Cadiz, Jerez and Seville in February; but Granada, surrounded by mountains, is apt to be chilly, and not long after leaving Cordova on the journey toward the north the mercury begins to drop. At Madrid snowdrifts in winter are not uncommon and the climate is like that of a city in our Northern States. All of Spain is very warm in summer, so that the best time for traveling through it is in the spring or fall.

Morocco and Algiers should certainly be visited in winter. Egypt is now visited by throngs in the late winter and early spring, but not many people go or stay there after April. Likewise the Holy Land and the Far East are best visited in winter or early spring.

If, then, the traveler had the time and money to change his climate like the birds, he would attain the maximum of comfort if he passed January and February in Northern Africa; March in Palestine and Turkey; April and May in Italy, Southern France and Spain; June in Paris and England; July and August in Switzerland, or Norway, Sweden and Russia; September in Germany; October in Austria; November in Greece; December in Sicily. Not that these are positively the best months for each country named, but that this might make the best circular tour for a year, from the climatic point of view.

Some of the principal sporting events, as well as others of interest, in the musical and social world, are thus summarized:

In Paris the Grand Prix is run on a Sunday early in June.

The Oxford-Cambridge boat race is rowed on the Thames near London, usually in March. The "eights' week" at Oxford comes in the middle of May; the Henley regatta late in June or July.

The cricket match between Oxford and Cambridge is played near the end of June, and between Eton and Harrow usually in July. As with us, football is a fall sport, but lasts later, games being played up to Christmas time. The Oxford-Cambridge match in 1896 took place Dec. 9.

Oxford is at its best during the Trinity term, from the middle of May to the middle of July; and Commemoration Week, usually the second or third in June, is the gayest.

The salons at Paris—there are now two of them—open in May and are kept open for some weeks. The Royal Academy in London is open from the first Monday in May to the first Monday in August.

When there is a Wagnerian festival at Bayreuth, it comes in mid-summer, but if you want to go you must write for tickets weeks and even months ahead; even then you may not get them. A letter addressed to the management at Bayreuth will procure the necessary information.

The fountains at Versailles generally play between 4 and 5 of the afternoon on the first Sunday of each month from May to October; those of St. Cloud at the same hour on the second Sunday of the month. The spectacle at Versailles costs about $2,000 and is well worth taking much pains to see.

The flower festival in the Bois de Boulogne at Paris comes about the time of the Grand Prix, early in June.

The Paris Exposition will open April 15 and close Nov. 5, 1900.

As to the ocean trip and the attendant expenses, Mr. Luce has this to say:

At the end of a trip every passenger on a trans-Atlantic steamer is supposed to give fees. It is an unwritten law, but as binding as the English constitution. The amount to be given always worries the novice, who dreads giving too little, and usually begrudges giving too much. If you give $2.50 to the man who waits on you at table, and a like amount to the man or woman who takes care of your stateroom, he or she will be perfectly satisfied; that much and no more is expected; if more is given, you are thought generous, but no benefit accrues to you, and often but slight benefit to the recipient, for frequently the receipts of all the stewards are pooled at the end of the trip and then divided equitably. So, in making a large gift, you but present so much money to the whole body of stewards.

For one, I see no reason why a head steward should be feed. It is virtually a duty to fee the under stewards, because their wages are small, in the expectation that they will receive enough from passengers to make their earnings reasonable. This is not the case with the head steward or anybody else on the ship. The men who frequent the smoking room usually make up a purse for the smoking room steward, but that is wholly a matter of generosity. The deck steward usually receives a small free from those who have frequently called upon him for services, and the passenger who is seasick usually calls upon him a good deal.

These hints for traveling on the Continent also come from the pen of the same author:

The only important difference between a first and second class compartment is that the first-class has either six or eight seats to a compartment, three or four looking front and three or four back—the second-class has ten, one more on each side. When all the seats are taken this is a slight disadvantage against the second-class, but that very rarely happens, not once in fifty rides. Indeed, there are seldom more than four people in a first or second-class compartment—or perhaps I would better say it is generally possible to find a compartment, if you wish, that has not more than two or three occupants. In several months' journeying, two of us had second-class compartments to ourselves more than two-thirds of the time, and never tipped the guard. That, however, might not be the case on the main lines of travel in July and August.

In cost the proportions, averaged from fares in many countries, are: First-class, one dollar; second-class, seventy-three cents; third-class, fifty-two cents. In other words, speaking in round numbers, first-class costs a third more than second; third-class a third less than second, and half as much as first.

The berths in European sleeping cars are even more uncomfortable than ours, and their cost makes it safe to lay down the rule never to travel by night if you can possibly help it. Some roads have first-class and second-class sleeping compartments. Bean tells me he has tried both, and finds no difference except in the price.

Usually tickets for the through trains are ten per cent. higher than those for accommodation trains, but the time saved is worth ten times the extra cost. What we should call the "limited" train from Rome to Naples takes five and one-fourth hours; the express, six and one-fourth, and the accommodation, eleven hourse. The distance is one hundred and sixty-two miles.

Bean, who always goes second-class, tells me that once he kept a record of every ticket bought while journeying twenty-seven hundred miles by short stages, and found he had averaged to pay $0.0266 a mile. On the same journey first-class fares would have averaged $0.0364 a mile; third-class, $0.189. On any one road, the price per mile is the same whether you travel five miles, fifty, or five hundred, except in the few regions where the zone system of rates prevails, and the ordinary traveler does find those.

The price of tickets is printed on the timetables hung up in the station, and in the timetable books that are issued.

Children travel free up to the age of three years throughout the greater part of the Continent; in Austria and Switzerland, up to two years. In Norway and Sweden half price is charged between three and twelve; in Austria and Switzerland, between two and ten. In Germany two children under ten travel on one ticket; a single child pays third-class fare to travel second; second-class to travel first. In Belgium three-quarters fare is charged for children from three to eight; in France, half fare from three to seven. When you are buying a ticket for a child, it is always advisable to let the ticket seller see the child.

From his experiences in traveling by boat Mr. Luce has arrived at the following deductions:

First-class tickets come much nearer being necessary on European steamboats than on European railways. As a rule the best accommodations on the boats are none too good. The best known boats, those crossing the English Channel, would not, for the most part, be tolerated on lines of equal importance in America; they draw only six or seven feet of water, which is one reason why they are so sure to make passengers seasick when the water is the least bit rough. But don't think that inevitable. I have crossed the channel when from one side to the other we could not see anything that properly could be called a wave.

On river and lake boats, before you get your ticket, wait to see what parts of the boat are allotted to first and second-class passengers, respectively. For an all-day ride, such as that on the Rhine, the freedom of the whole boat given by a first-class ticket is in any event desirable. On the Lake of Thun the second-class accommodations are for sight seeing and pleasure much superior to those allotted the first-class passengers, who usually crowd forward into the second-class seats, in spite of their tickets; but on the Lake of Brienz, only a mile or so away, the second-class accommodations are miserable. On Lake Geneva it costs one dollar and fifty cents to go from end to end of the lake first-class; sixty cents second class, and in pleasant weather the second-class seats are better, being ahead of the smoke-stack and giving the finer views.

Referring to bicycling, Mr. Luce is authority for the following statements:

There are many flinty roads in England, especially south of London, and though France has the best highways in the world, they are made of flinty material and demand good tires to stand the strain. Many riders have found it desirable to reinforce their tires by a strip of rubber going round the tire where the most wear comes, say an inch and a half wide. It may cost $3 to have this put on. Only the rash wheelman will make a foreign trip without a tire repair outfit, or at least a supply of tape to cover a puncture till a repair shop can be reached. Yet many a returning rider will report having gone through Europe without a single puncture.

The brick roads of Holland are disliked by some wheelmen—praised by others. As in Holland more than in most other countries, the villages and rural districts are the more picturesque and the less spoiled by the quick-tour people, and as there are absolutely no hills to climb, it is surely worth the wheelman's attention. "The roads of Spain," declares one bicycler, "are good, as a rule, though not equal to those in France and Italy. A trip through any one of our States would be a more formidable undertaking than one through Spain. Of course we attracted universal attention, but it was always accompanied by courteous respect." Normandy is another delightful region for bicycling, and Touraine is declared a paradise for wheelmen. In Northern France the climate in summer is excellent for the sport, being much less wet than that of England, and averaging considerably cooler than that of the United States.

A favorite trip is from Rotterdam or Amsterdam up the Rhine Valley to Switzerland, and then from Geneva straight to Paris and the sea. Home-coming wheelmen who had just made this trip told me, however, that if they were to do it again, they would reverse it, so as to slide down the Rhine Valley rather than climb it. Such a trip from New York to New York, with first-class passage on a slow line, could handily be made in two months, at a total cost of from two to three hundred dollars, according to the hotel accommodations demanded. By crossing second-class and economizing on the other side, it can be done for $150 or even less, but most people would not enjoy what they would get for an expenditure of under $200.

The postal systems abroad leave little perplexity for the bicycle tourist in the matter of luggage. He is almost sure to want more than he can well carry on his wheel, but large parcels are sent by post at comparatively slight cost, and a valise can be mailed with the certainty that it will reach your destination before you can get there on your wheel, unless you are to go but a very short distance. The notion of mailing a heavy valise for 20 cents or so strikes Americans with a force that they remember when they get home and wonder whether our own postal department does for us quite all it might.

Referring again to the fee system the writer says:

If the chambermaid does for you anything outside her routine work, she should get a fee, always small; otherwise, ignore her when she lies in wait for you ás you descend the hotel stairs the last time.

The declaration of too many tourists that you must fee everybody in a European hotel is all nonsense. The porter and the waiter are the indispensables, and so with the baggage porter, if you have trunks or let him black your boots. The others are mere charities.

As to amounts, the general rule is ten per cent. of the bill if you stay but one night or take a single meal. This applies whether the bill is twenty cents or two dollars or twenty dollars. A penny in the shilling is all that English waiters expect; ten centimes (or two cents) in the franc all that French waiters expect. Where a hotel bill is above two dollars, a percentage as low as five per cent. may be given without surprise. On paying a bill of five dollars at a hotel it would be the usual thing to give the waiter twenty cents, the portier twenty cents, and the chambermaid five cents. On paying eight dollars, you might give no more and no comment would be even looked; or you might make it thirty cents for the waiter, the same for the portier, and five or ten cents for the chambermaid.

Never pay any fees until your bill is presented. You are not expected to dole out the pennies or francs from meal to meal, or, indeed, at any time before you go away.

Look at it purely as a matter of business. If you haven't the change, make the waiter or the porter or whoever you want to fee, get your money changed, and give what you meant to give, no more. In an American hotel that would be thought stingy; abroad it is thought the natural thing.

The idea that even servants in private houses must be feed is the most repugnant of all to American instincts. Yet go to an English mansion of rank for even a stay from Saturday to Monday, and you are expected to remember the butler and the footman to the tune of a dollar or so.

In pensions, ten per cent. of the bills would be an unusual distribution. If you stay several weeks, five per cent. will be a great plenty, and two or three per cent. is probably nearer the common thing.

Cab drivers are usually made happy by ten per cent., though in such a place as Naples, where the prescribed fare is abnormally low (fourteen cents), to give a lira, twenty cents, is frequent.

In museums and galleries, fees of ten cents predominate. It is always safe to start on that; if more is the custom, don't fear that you will not be told of it.

Mr. Luce's experiences with the cab system in Europe as he has found it is thus explained:

In the cities the cab and omnibus play a much more important part than on this side of the water. Cab hire is ridiculously cheap on the Continent, and all well-to-do people, natives as well as foreigners, make habitual use of the cab. The prescribed rates are to be found on a card in every vehicle, and therefore no advance bargain is necessary so long as you keep inside the city limits; but plan an excursion into the country and a bargain in advance should always be made. The charge is almost invariably according to the nature of the vehicle or the distance traveled—not in proportion to the number of occupants. Two people, and often three, can ride as cheap as one person, but since four or more people require a larger cab or two horses, there is a larger fare. It is the invariable custom to fee the driver—five cents being the average tip on short drives. In Naples, where the regulations let the drivers charge only fourteen cents to go anywhere in the city limits, a lira (twenty cents), would usually be given to the driver, but if you gave him only sixteen or eighteen cents he would not seriously demur. Throughout most of Europe you may reckon on giving twenty to thirty cents for a cab fare, with four or five cents as pourboire.

How exact Mr. Luce may be in the details I cannot say, but he gives the following information as to certain articles which an American may have with him and find dutiable in various countries:

Dutiable goods in Great Britain are tobacco, wines, liquors, tea, coffee, cocoa and Florida water. American reprints of English works and copyright music are absolutely confiscated. Firearms and ammunition cannot be landed in Ireland, unless declared to customs and will then be detained until a magistrate's warrant to carry them has been granted.

In France, tobacco, wines and liquors are subject to duty. Matches are strictly prohibited and liable to confiscation, as also tobacco, except small quantities for personal use. Household goods and wearing apparel admitted free, with but few if any questions asked. The penalty for false declarations is heavy.

In Germany, Switzerland, Italy and Belgium the only articles subject to duty which travelers would be likely to carry are tobacco and spirits, and on these the duty is trifling.

These reflections on shopping in Europe may prove of interest to some travelers:

It is chiefly by reason of specialties that European shopping can rightfully attract American buyers, not alone because special application to any one industry by a large part of the people of a locality is sure to make its price cheap, but also because an excess of production results in greater latitude for selection. Geneva may again illustrate, for besides watches, it makes a specialty of music boxes, and nowhere else can you find such a variety at such cheap prices. Of other specialties the tourist will do well to buy—

Tortoise shell, coral and lava in Naples.

Wood carving in Switzerland, the Black Forest, Sorrento, Norway and Sweden.

Silks in Genoa, Milan and Lyons.

Silver and gold filagree work in Genoa.

Cameos, mosaics and many other kinds of ornaments in Florence, Venice and Rome—Florence being the cheapest.

Pearls and turquoises in Rome and Florence.

Gloves in Naples, Genoa, Milan and Paris.

Artificial flowers in Paris.

Laces in Antwerp, Brussels, Venice and Seville.

Venetian glass, of course, in Venice.

Umbrellas in Milan or Switzerland.

Toilet articles—soaps, perfumes, sponges, etc.—in the German cities and in Paris.

Silk underwear, Sorrento and Milan.

Cutlery, old silverware, and Sheffield plate, in London.

Engravings and all reproductions, in Berlin.

The cheaper stones—amethysts, topaz, cairngorns, etc.—in Switzerland and Scotland.

It will be noticed that in the foregoing list the names of Italian cities predominate. It is the general rule abroad that as you go south, prices drop. The easier it is to live, the lower the price the workman will take. And the easier it is to live, the more children and so the more competition for work. That is why Italy abounds in bargains.

These hints as to postal matter may also prove available:

All European countries, as well as the United States and Canada, are now in the Postal Union, and the rates from any one country to any other are virtually the same corresponding in the coinage of the country in question to the following on mail matter sent from the United States:—

Letters, each half ounce............ 5 cts.

Postal cards .... 2 cts.
Newpapers, books and other printed
    matter, each two ounces.......... 1 ct.
Commercial papers:
    Packets not in excess of ten ounces
        for each two ounces or fraction
        thereof .... 5 cts.
    Packets in excess of ten ounces, for
        each two ounces or fraction thereof 1 ct.
Samples of merchandise:
    Packets not in excess of four ounces. 2 cts.
    Packets in excess of four ounces, for
        each two ounces or fraction thereof 10 cts.
    Registration fee on letters or other
        articles .... 10 cts.

In his most comprehensive little work on European travel Mr. Luce forgets nothing and even includes these words of advice to the devote of the camera:

It is often thought that in buying a camera the securing of a good lens is the all important thing, and that the mechanism of the shutter is a minor detail. Bean didn't think so when his shutter refused to work in the Alhambra, a place of all places where a camera in good condition seemed most desirable. It turned out that the wooden base of the shutter mechanism had been swollen during the ocean voyage so that something was thrown out of gear, and a camera that had done long and excellent work in America was for a while not worth a cent. Nobody could be found with knowledge enough of hand cameras to repair this one, and it was weeks before Bean's own struggle with the thing in spare moments got that shutter into condition again. Moral: Have your camera thoroughly examined by an expert in such matters before you start.

Wherever there is a film agency, you can get your films developed, but the foreign work in this line is not equal to the American, and it is better to wait till you get back. Yet it is wise to have one or two films developed now and then to see that the shutter is working right and that the film has not been damaged.

CHAPTER XVII.

The Paris Exposition of 1900.

UNDER this head F. O. Houghton & Co., steamship agents, of No. 115 State street, Boston, have compiled in the following comprehensive form considerable information as to this coming event which is casting such a mighty shadow before it:

SITE OF THE EXPOSITION.

Preparations for the Exposition are now well advanced. The preliminary studies are made with great care and thoroughness, and the general scheme of the Exposition is now well defined. The works of demolition and construction, for which the period of a little more than two years remaining will barely suffice, have begun and will be vigorously prosecuted. The Exposition will open April 15, and will close Nov. 5, 1900. The site will comprise the public grounds on both sides of the Seine from the Place de la Concorde, which is the centre of the city, to a point beyond the Pont d'Jena, embracing the Champ de Mars, the Trocadero Palace and Park (site of the Exposition of 1889), the Esplanade des Invalides, the Quai d'Orsay, the Quai de la Conference, the Cour la Reine, and a large section of the Champs Elysees, including the site of the Palais de l'Industrie, the great building erected for the International Exposition of 1855, the first of the series. No other city in the world contains, in its very centre, an equal area available for a great exposition. This site leaves nothing to be desired in point of convenience, and lends itself admirably to the works of decoration and embellishment, in which the French people are past masters.

ARCHITECTURAL PLANS.

The unique Palace of the Trocadero, erected for the Exposition of 1878, and utilized a second time in 1889, will be used, as well as several of the great exposition halls of 1889 in the Champ de Mars, but all of them will undergo more or less modification. The Eiffel Tower will be preserved, but it is probable that some new and striking features will be added to it.

TRANSPORTATION FACILITIES, HOTELS. ETC.

The national and municipal authorities and the management of the Exposition are preparing to co-operate in improving the transportation facilities and public conveniences of Paris, and in adding, before 1900, to the already numerous attractions of the city. A number of modern hotels, some of which are already under construction, and several handsome new theatres will be built, and the magnificent Opera Comique, now in course of erection, will be completed. Public parks, gardens and squares will be created in all parts of the city. At night the city will be brilliantly illuminated by an extensive system of electric lights as far as the outer boulevards and including the Bois de Boulogne and de Vincennes.

It is the avowed purpose to make the Exposition surpass all its predecessors, both in France and elsewhere; not, perhaps, in extent or in architectural features, for it is conceded that in these respects there is little hope of eclipsing the great achievement at Chicago, but in its artistic aspects, in the logical, comprehensive and scientific system of classification and award, and in the uniformity and harmony of the whole.

GENERAL PROJECT.

The first international exposition was held in 1855, the second in 1867, and the third and fourth, respectively, in 1878 and 1889. The interval between the first and second was twelve years; eleven years separated the second and third, and a like period the third and fourth. The Exposition of 1889 was scarcely terminated when the public opinion of France spontaneously fixed 1900, the closing year of the century, then eleven years distant, as the date of its successor.

FINANCIAL ARRANGEMENTS.

One hundred million francs ($20,000,000) was provided as a guaranty fund for the Exposition. Of this amount, 20,000,000 francs was appropriated by the National Government, and 20,000,000 francs by the city of Paris, while 60,000,000 francs represent the net proceeds of an emission of 3,250,000 bonds of 20 francs each. These bonds were issued by the Government, with the co-operation of five leading financial institutions, the Credit Lyonnais, the Credit Foncier, the Comptoir National d'Escompte, the Societe Generale pour Favoriser le Development de Commerce et de l'Industrie en France, and the Societe Generale de Credit Industriel et Commercial. These institutions underwrote bonds to the amount of 2,400,000 francs, and receive a commission of 5 per cent. on the sales. After providing for this commission and for the other expenses of the issue, there remain 60,000,000 francs, which are deposited at the Caisse des Depots et Consignations until 1900 at 2½ per cent. interest, the Bank of France agreeing to make advances from time to time for preliminary expenses to the amount of 6,000,000 francs at 1¼ per cent. interest, upon the security of receipts of the Caisse des Depots et Consignations for deposits of the profits of the bonds.

Any surplus that may remain after the expenses of the Exposition are defrayed will be divided equally between the national and municipal treasuries.

ADMISSIONS.

The regular price for the afternoon will be one franc (19.3 cents). For mornings, afternoons and special days the admission price may be increased. Season and monthly tickets will be offered at a reduction. Every exhibitor in the contemporary exposition will be given a complimentary season ticket, and the necessary employees at his exhibit will also receive complimentary admissions.

PROTECTION OF EXHIBITS.

No work of art or exhibit of any kind can be copied or reproduced except by a special permit of the exhibitor, approved by the administration. The taking of general photographs, however, will be authorized. Inventions susceptible of being patented, plans and specifications of machinery, etc., will be fully protected.

CATALOGUES.

A general catalogue will be prepared in the French language, naming the works and productions of all nations on exhibition, with the names of exhibitors and the location of exhibits in the buildings or grounds. The sale of these catalogues on the exposition grounds will be regulated by the administration and will be subject to the payment of a royalty.

RECOMPENSES, DIPLOMAS, ETC.

All works exhibited will be passed upon, as

in 1889, by an international jury, which will have three degrees of jurisdiction—juries of class, juries of group, superior jury.

Reports will be published by the Government, together with an official list of the awards.

Only diplomas will be granted as recompenses. They will be thus classified: grand prize diplomas, gold medal diplomas, silver medal diplomas, bronze medal diplomas, honorable mention diplomas.

No exhibitor acting as a juror and no firm or company represented on a jury by any member, stockholder, agent or employe, will be eligible to an award.

CONCESSIONS.

Concessions and privileges for entertainments, refreshment booths, etc., will be granted by the Minister of Commerce, Industry, Posts and Telegraphs upon the recommendation of the Commissary General. All privileges for pecuniary benefit must pay a royalty or percentage of receipts to the exposition. No advertisements, catalogues or prospectuses can be circulated in the exposition grounds except under special license, for which a suitable fee will be charged.

REGULATIONS AS TO TARIFF DUTIES, ETC.

The exposition grounds are constituted a bonded warehouse. Foreign exhibits may enter France through any custom house. They should be accompanied by a bulletin from the shipper, attached to the bill of lading and indicating their nature, class, weight and place of origin. These goods will be transported directly to the exposition grounds under the conditions of international or domestic transit at the choice of the shipper. They will be exempt from statistical dues and from inspection at the frontier. Seals will be affixed without charge. All foreign products will be taken in charge at the exposition grounds by the special customs agents, and, if finally entered for consumption, will be subject only, whatever their origin, to the duties imposed upon like products from the most favored nation.

CLASSIFICATION OF EXHIBITS.

The post of honor is occupied by education—"the channel by which man enters into life, the source of all progress." Next come works of art, and the third place is assigned to the instruments and general processes of letters, sciences and arts. Then come "the great factors of contemporary production, the most powerful agents of industrial achievement at the end of the nineteenth century," the material and general processes of mechanics, electricity, civil engineering, methods of transportation.

A new group has been created for the "moral and material work of colonization," and the series closes with the military and naval group.

In all there will be eighteen groups and one hundred and twenty sections, as compared with twelve groups and nearly a thousand sections at Chicago.

The government at Washington is now endeavoring to secure, in behalf of the League of American Wheelmen, the free entry of bicycles into European countries. On Oct. 27, 1897, Secretary Sherman sent the following letter to the American ambassador, at Paris, and similar letters to the United States embassies at Rome and Berlin, and to the Legations at Berne and Brussels:

Sir: I enclose herewith a copy of a letter addressed to me under date of October 15, by Isaac B. Potter, President of the League of American Wheelmen, in which he represents the important standing of that organization, enrolling as it does, 100,000 associates, the number of its members who visit the European countries for recreation and the desirability of having that organization placed in those countries upon the same or similar footing of reciprocal privilege with other well-known associations of touring cyclists.

It is presumed that the facilities accorded in France to the British organization and others on the continent have been reached by virtue of a reciprocal understanding whereby the formalities for the respective introduction of cycles and the favors shown to the members have been specified.

You are authorized to bring the matter informally at first, and afterward more formally, should a suitable occasion for such a course appear, to the notice of the Government of France, expressing the pleasure it would afford this Government to see a convenient and equitable interchange of courtesies established in this regard. Should you find a disposition to favorably consider this suggestion you will ascertain upon what terms the proposed arrangement might be effected. Respectfully yours,
JOHN SHERMAN.

Meanwhile Joseph Pennell, the L. A. W. representative in London, has been for weeks pursuing the same object, and a letter has just been received by President Potter from Mr. Pennell announcing that the Swiss and Belgian governments have decided to grant the application of the L. A. W. and it only remains to make out the necessary papers. A letter has also been received from the embassy at Rome reporting favorable progress and asking for a quantity of "sample" membership tickets of the L. A. W. for use among the Italian customs stations. A further report is expected.

The splendor of the last Paris Exposition is undoubted. Yet its success was attained in spite of the fact that it commemorated the fall of the Bastile, which did not make it too popular with other European countries which favored forms of government other than republican. In 1900 no such adverse circumstance will militate against its success and it is sure to be witnessed by hundreds of thousands of English-speaking persons, ready to welcome the dawn of a new century.

More Details of the Exposition.

The World Almanac, which we quote by permision, has among pages of other matter of details on the subject, these interesting facts:

THE JURY.

The jury will be, as in 1889, international, sub-divided into juries of class, juries of groups, and superior jury. Foreign jurors will be named by the Commissioners of the respective countries. The Foreign Commissioners will be ex officio members of the superior jury. The superior jury will finally revise the list of awards, and the distribution of diplomas will take place about the beginning of September, 1900.

AWARDS.

Only diplomas will be granted, thus classified: Grand prize diplomas, gold medal diplomas, silver medal diplomas, and diplomas of honorable mention.

MAIN FEATURES.

The grand entrance to the Exposition of 1900 will be off the Place de la Concorde, close to the Seine, but there will be a multitude of other entrances in the Champs-Elysees, the Champs de Mars, and the Esplanade des Invalides. The Exposition authorities themeslves do not know what will be the most popular and striking feature of the Exposition, but it will doubtless prove to be one of the following, all of them novel and attractive:

1. The street of modern Paris, running along the embankment from the Place de la Concorde to the Pont de l'Alma. This will illustrate the art and wit of France and will contain palaces of dancing, song, and all that is refined in the curiosities of Paris. The directors of the Opera and another leading Paris theatre are engaged upon its elaboration.

2. M. Deloncle's telescope, bringing the moon's surface apparently within 40 kilometres (25 miles) of the spectator.

3. A city of gold, near the Trocadero, showing every detail of gold production, with Californian miners and models of the mines.

4. A gigantic Turning Palace, or Revolving Tower, 100 yards high and lighted throughout by electricity.

5. The Grand and Little Palaces of the Fine Arts of all nations.

6. The Pavilion of the Press, and those of the special commissioners which will be scattered over the area.

7. An enormous Terrestrial Globe by the famous French geographer, M. Reclus, placed, owing to its size, outside the Exposition proper.

8. Palace of the Army and Navy and a Palace of Food, or Alimentation.

WOMAN'S PALACE.

In addition to these there will almost certainly be a Woman's Palace, showing the development of feminine education, training and labor; a switchback; a colossal vat; an enormous bell; imitation of the Blue Grotto of Capri, of the fountain of Vancluse; captive balloons; a cyclorama of the war of secession in America, and other devices to interest, charm, or amuse.

THE EXTENT.

It is calculated that the Exposition of 1900 will cover three times the space occupied by the exhibition of 1889. The ground will not be partitioned off by nationalities, but by sections, each section being devoted to a particular industry or art.

CONCESSIONS.

In most cases the system adopted for the disposal of concessions will be auction sales and special contracts; and all applications for concessions for the right to establish shows of various kinds should be addressed by the American citizen to Major Handy, Chicago. In all concessions there will be inserted the following clauses and general conditions:

1. No one may bid for a concession unless he is domiciled in Paris or has a qualified and responsible agent there.

2. The applicant must prove that he is possessed of the necessary means and is capable of carrying his undertaking to a successful issue.

3. The applicant must make a deposit in accordance with the decree relating to all agreements signed in the name of the State.

4. Concessionaires must build and install their shows, etc., at their own expense and at their own risk and peril, and must submit plans of their buildings to the administration of the exhibition on or before the —— day of ——.

5. Water, gas, and electricity will be supplied by the exhibition at ordinary prices.

6. All shows, exhibitions, and establishments directed by concessionaires must be open to the public throughout

the duration of the exhibition (from April 15 to November 5, 1900), and from the opening to the closing of the gates.

7. Precautions against fire must be taken by concessionaires at their own expense.

8. No concession may be sub-let in whole or in part without the sanction of the Commissary-General.

9. Cases of disagreement between concessionaires and the administration will be referred to a jury of three members, one to be designated by the Commissary-General, the second by the concessionaire, and the third by the other two.

The Fleet of Transatlantic Passenger Steamers.

Includes only regular passenger lines from New York. Offices and piers are in Manhattan Borough unless otherwise stated.

Steamship	Built Year	Built Place	Builders	Tonnage Net	Tonnage Gross	Horse Power Indicated	Horse Power Developed	Commander	Length	Breadth	Depth
NEW YORK AND GLASGOW, Pier foot W. 21st St.			**ALLAN-STATE LINE.** (Office, 53 Broadway.)					**STATE LINE ESTABLISHED 1872.**			
State of Nebraska	1880	Glasgow	Lond. & Gl'gowCo.,Ld	3580	8144	..	..	Brown	385	43	32
Mongolia	1891	Glasgow	Lond. & Gl'gowCo.,Ld	3080	4750	..	..	Braes	400	46	33.6
State of California	1891	Glasgow	Lond. & Gl'gowCo.,Ld	3670	4500	..	..	......	386	46	29.7
NEW YORK AND SOUTHAMPTON, Pier foot Fulton St., N. R.			**AMERICAN LINE.** (Office, 6 Bowling Green.)					**ESTABLISHED 1892.**			
St. Louis	1894	Philadelphia	Wm. Cramp & Sons	5894	11629	20000	..	Randle	535.8	63	43
St. Paul	1894	Philadelphia	Wm. Cramp & Sons	5874	11629	20000	..	Jamison	535.8	63	43
Paris	1889	Glasgow	J. & G. Thomson	5289	10795	20000	9000	Watkins	580	63.8	42
New York	1888	Glasgow	J. & G. Thomson	6318	10603	20000	9000	Passow	580	63.8	42
NEW YORK AND GLASGOW, Pier foot W. 24th St.			**ANCHOR LINE.** (Office, 7 Bowling Green.)					**ESTABLISHED 1852.**			
City of Rome	1881	Barrow	Barrow S. B. Co	3468	8144	..	1500	Young	561	53	37
Anchoria	1874	Barrow	Barrow S. B. Co	2713	4168	..	617	John Wilson	408	40	34
Bolivia	1872	Port Glasgow	R. Duncan & Co	2626	4050	..	1120	Baxter	400	40	35
Circassia	1878	Barrow	Barrow S. B. Co	2170	4272	..	600	Bothby	400	42	35
Ethiopia	1873	Glasgow	A. Stephen & Son	2604	4005	..	720	Wadsworth	402	42	35
Furnessia	1880	Barrow	Barrow S. B. Co	3613	5495	..	600	Harris	445	45	35
NEW YORK, QUEENSTOWN, AND LIVERPOOL, Pier foot Clarkson St.			**CUNARD LINE.** (Office, 4 Bowling Green.)					**ESTABLISHED 1840.**			
Campania	1892	Fairfield	John Elder & Co	5000	12950	30000	*	Walker	620	65.3	43
Lucania	1892	Fairfield	John Elder & Co	5000	12950	30000	*	H. McKay	620	65.3	43
Etruria	1885	Fairfield	John Elder & Co	3257	7718	14500	2500	Ferguson	501.6	57.2	38.2
Umbria	1884	Fairfield	John Elder & Co	3345	7718	14500	2500	Dutton	501.6	57.2	38.2
Aurania	1883	Glasgow	J. & G. Thomson	4029	7268	8500	1500	A. McKay	470	57.2	37.2
Servia	1881	Glasgow	J. & G. Thomson	3971	7391	10000	1000	Watt	515	52	37
Gallia	1879	Glasgow	J. & G. Thomson	3061	4808	4500	700	Warr	430.1	44.6	34.4
NEW YORK AND HAVRE, Pier foot Morton St.			**FRENCH LINE.** (Office, 3 Bowling Green.)					**ESTABLISHED 1860.**			
La Touraine	1890	St. Nazaire	CieGleTransatlan'que	..	9778	12000	..	Santelli	536	55	38
La Gascogne	1886	Toulon	Soc. des Forges, etc	4158	7416	9000	..	Baudelon	508	52	38
La Bourgogne	1886	Toulon	Soc. des Forges, etc	4171	7400	9000	..	Le Boeuf	508	52	38
La Champagne	1886	St. Nazaire	CieGleTransatlan'que	3906	7110	9000	..	Poirot	508	51	38
La Bretagne	1886	St. Nazaire	CieGleTransatlan'que	3889	7010	9000	..	Rupé	508	51	38
La Normandie	1882	Barrow, Eng.	......	3475	6112	6500	..	Deloncle	459	50	34
NEW YORK, SOUTHAMPTON, CHERBOURG, AND HAMBURG, Pier foot 1st St., Hoboken.			**HAMBURG-AMERICAN LINE.** (Office, 37 Broadway.)					**ESTABLISHED 1847.**			
Fürst Bismarck	1890	Stettin	Vulcan S. B. Co	..	13000	16400	2800	Albers	520	57	40
Normannia	1890	Glasgow	Fairfield S. B. Co	..	12000	16000	2750	Barends	520	57	40
Augusta Victoria	1889	Stettin	Vulcan S. B. Co	..	12000	13500	3500	Kaempff	520	56	38
Columbia	1889	Birkenhead	Laird Bros	..	10000	12500	2500	Vogelgesang	460	55	38
Pennsylvania	1897	Belfast	Harland & Wolff	..	225	9	6000	Spliedt	560	62	42
Pretoria	1897	Hamburg	Blohm & Voss	..	13500	6000	..	Kopff	560	62	42
Palatia	1894	Stettin	Vulcan S. B. Co	..	8000	5000	..	Karlowa	460	52	32
Patria	1894	..c..		..	8000	5000	..	Bauer	460	52	32
Phoenicia	1894	Hamburg	Blohm & Voss	..	8000	5500	..	Leithauser	460	52	32
Prussia	1894	Belfast	Harland & Wolff	..	7000	5000	..	Schmidt	446	51	30
Persia	1894	Belfast	Harland & Wolff	..	7000	5000	..	Reessing	446	51	30
Armenia	1896	Newcastle	Palmers	..	7000	3000	..	Magin	400	50	30
Arcadia	1896	Belfast	Harland & Wolff	..	7000	3000	..	Martens	400	49	30
Arabia	1896	Belfast	Harland & Wolff	..	7000	3000	..	Pietsch	400	49	30
Asturia	1896	Newcastle	Palmers	..	7000	3000	..	Kuhn	394	49	30
Andalusia	1896	Belfast	Palmers	..	7000	3000	..	Schroeder	400	50	30
Adria	1896	Newcastle	Palmers	..	7000	3000	..	Reuter	400	50	30
Ambria	1896	Flensburg	Flensburg S. B. Co	..	5043	5000	..	Froehlich	404	32	25
Alesia	1896	Flensburg	Flensburg S. B. Co	..	5050	5000	..	Krech	404	32	25
Aragonia	1896	Flensburg	Flensburg S. B. Co	..	5250	5000	..	H. Schmidt	404	32	25
NEW YORK, BOULOGNE, AMSTERDAM, AND ROTTERDAM, Piers foot 5th and 7th Sts., Hoboken.			**HOLLAND-AMERICA LINE.** NETHERLANDS-AMERICAN LINE (Office, 39 Broadway.)					**ESTABLISHED 1874.**			
Rotterdam	1897	Belfast	Harland & Wolff	..	5000	5000	..	Bonjer	485	53	34
Spaarndam	1881	Belfast	Harland & Wolff	..	3123	4539	..	3500	Van der Zee	430	43	31
Maasdam	1872	Belfast	Harland & Wolff	..	2702	3984	..	3500	Ald. Potjer	420	41	31
Veendam	1872	Belfast	Harland & Wolff	..	2438	3707	..	3500	Stenger	420	41	31
Werkendam	1881	Belfast	Harland & Wolff	..	2654	3657	..	2500	Ponsen	410	39	29
Amsterdam	1879	Belfast	Harland & Wolff	..	2681	3627	..	2500	W. Bakker	411	39	29
Obdam	1880	Belfast	Harland & Wolff	..	2277	3558	..	2500	Roggeveen	411	39	29
Edam	1878	Belfast	Harland & Wolff	..	2361	3329	..	2100	Bruinsma	390	38	29
Statendam †		Belfast	Harland & Wolff	..	7600	10500	..	5500	......	525	60	43

* 26,500 registered.   † Building.

Steamships	Built.		Builders.	Tonnage.		Horse Power.		Commander.	Dimensions in Feet.		
	Year.	Place.		Net.	Gross.	Indicated.	Regis Grctd.		Length.	Breadth.	Depth.
NEW YORK, SOUTHAMPTON, AND BREMEN, Pier 2d St., Hoboken.			NORTH GERMAN LLOYD. (Office, 2 Bowling Green.)						ESTABLISHED 1857.		
Kaiser Wilhelm d. Grosse	1897	Stettin	Vulcan Shipb'ld'g Co.	..	13800	27000	...	Englehart	649	66	43
Kaiser Friedrich*	..	Danzig	Schichau Shipbl'g Co.	..	12800	25000	...	Stormer	600	64	41
Spree	1890	Stettin	Vulcan Shipb'ld'g Co.	3769	6963	13000	...	Meier	481	52	58
Havel	1890	Stettin	Vulcan Shipb'ld'g Co.	3769	6963	13000	...	Christoffers	481	52	38
Lahn	1887	Fairfield	Fairfield E. & S. B. Co.	2879	5581	8800	...	Pohle	464	49	37
Saale	1886	Glasgow	Elder & Co.	2779	5381	7500	...	Blanke	455	48	36
Trave	1886	Glasgow	Elder & Co.	2779	5831	7500	...	Thalenhorst	455	48	36
Aller	1886	Glasgow	Elder & Co.	2779	5381	7500	...	Wettin	455	48	36
Ems	1884	Glasgow	Elder & Co.	2293	5192	7000	...	Harrassowitz	445	47	35
Freidrich d. Grosse	1896	Stettin	Vulcan Shipb'ld'g Co.	..	10500	7000	...	Eichel	546	60	35
Königin Luise	1896	Stettin	Vulcan Shipb'ld'g Co.	..	10500	7000	...	v. Schuck'nn	544	60	35
Barbarossa	1896	Hamburg	Blohm & Voss	..	10500	7000	...	Richter	546	60	35
Bremen	1896	Danzig	Schichau Shipbl'g Co.	..	10500	8000	...	Reinkasten	544	60	35
H. H. Meier	1892	Newcastle	Mitchell, A'strong Co.	..	5306	3800	...	Steencken	481	48	29
NEW YORK AND GENOA, Pier foot 2d St., Hoboken.			NORTH GERMAN LLOYD. (Office, 2 Bowling Green.)						ESTABLISHED 1892.		
Fulda	1883	Glasgow	Elder & Co.	..	4814	6300	...	Petermann	445	46	36
Werra	1882	Glasgow	Elder & Co.	..	4815	6300	...	Mirow	445	46	38
Kaiser Wilhelm II	1888	Stettin	Vulcan Shipb'ld'g Co.	4776	6930	6500	...	Hogemann	465	52	27
NEW YORK AND ANTWERP, Pier foot Fulton St., N. R.			RED STAR LINE. (Office, 6 Bowling Green.)						ESTABLISHED 1873.		
Friesland	1889	Glasgow	J. & G. Thomson	5023	682.	..	800	Nickels	455	51	38
Westernland	1883	Birkenhead	Laird Bros	4320	5994	..	700	Mills	455	47	35
Noordland	1883	Birkenhead	Laird Bros	4019	5398	..	500	Loesewitz	419	47	35
Southwark	1893	Dumbarton	W. Denny & Bros	5642	8607	..	1237	Bence	494	57	37
Kensington	1894	Glasgow	J. & G. Thomson	5645	8669	..	1237	Bond	494	57	37
NEW YORK, CHRISTIANIA, COPENHAGEN, AND STETTIN, Pier foot 4th St., Hoboken.			THINGVALLA LINE. (Office, 28 State St.)						ESTABLISHED 1879.		
Amerika	1872	Belfast	Harland & Wolff	..	3367	4000	..	Thomsen	437	41	31
Hekla	1884	Greenock	Scott & Co	..	3258	2150	..	Laub	333	41	29
Island	1882	Copenhagen	Burmeister & Wain	..	2844	2000	..	Skjodt	324	39	29
Norge	1881	Glasgow	Stephens & Son	..	8359	1600	..	Knudsen	340	41	32
Thingvalla	1874	Copenhagen	Burmeister & Wain	..	2524	1000	..	Berentsen	301	37	21
NEW YORK, QUEENSTOWN, AND LIVERPOOL, Pier foot W. 10th St.			WHITE STAR LINE. (Office, 9 Broadway.)						ESTABLISHED 1870.		
Teutonic	1889	Belfast	Harland & Wolff	4269	9984	16000	2400	Cameron	565	57	39
Majestic	1889	Belfast	Harland & Wolff	4269	9965	16000	2400	E. J. Smith	565	57	39
Britannic	1874	Belfast	Harland & Wolff	3152	5004	4590	760	Haddock	455	45	33
Germanic	1874	Belfast	Harland & Wolff	2989	5065	4500	760	McKinstry	455	45	33
Adriatic	1871	Belfast	Harland & Wolff	2458	3887	3500	600		437	40	31
Oceanic *	..	Belfast	Harland & Wolff	...	17000	..	..		704		
NEW YORK AND LONDON, Wilson Pier, Brooklyn Borough.			WILSON'S & FURNESS-LEYLAND LINE. (Office, 22 State St.)						ESTABLISHED 1896.		
Alexandra	1897	Glasgow	Stephens & Son	..	10000	..	..	Marshall	490	52.3	34.6
Boadicea	1897	Glasgow	Stephens & Son	..	10000	..	..		490	52.3	34.6
Cleopatra	1897	Hull	Earl S. B. & Eng. Co.	..	10000	..	..	Brown	490	52.3	34.6
Winifred	1897	Belfast	Harland & Wolff	..	10000	..	..		490	52.3	34.6
Victoria	1897	W. Hartlep'l	Furness, Withy & Co.	..	10000	..	..	Farrington	490	52.3	34.6
NEW YORK AND HULL, Wilson Pier, Brooklyn Borough.			WILSON LINE. (Office, 22 State St.)						ESTABLISHED 1840.		
Buffalo	1885	Newcastle	Palmers	2909	4431	..	600	Malet	385	46	28
Ohio	1880	Dumbarton	A. McMill & Sons	2557	3967	..	450	Akester	360	43	28
Colorado	1887	Hull	Earles	2787	4220	..	600	Whitton	370	45	28
Martello	1884	Hull	Earles	2424	3709	..	550	Potter	370	42	28
Francisco	1891	Newcastle	R. Stephenson & Co. Ld	2971	4604	..	600	Jenkins	370	47	28
Hindoo	1889	Newcastle	R. Stephenson & Co. Ld	2407	3720	..	500	Wing	365	43	28

*Building.

TIME AND DISTANCE REQUIRED TO STOP STEAMERS.

The following calculations as to the length of time and distance required to stop a steam vessel going full speed ahead when the propelling machinery is reversed were made by W. D. Weaver, late Assistant Engineer of the United States Navy, for London *Engineer*. Omitting the mathematical formulas, Mr. Weaver's conclusions are given for the Cunarder Etruria, the Italian ironclad Lepanto, the United States naval vessels Columbia, Yorktown, Bancroft, and Cushing, and the Russian torpedo boat Wiborg:

	Displacement.	Horse Power.	Speed.	Distance.	Time.
				Feet.	Seconds.
Etruria	9,680	14,321	20.18	2,464	167
Lepanto	4,680	15,040	18	2,522	192
Columbia	7,350	17,991	22.8	2,147	135
Yorktown	1,700	3,205	16.14	989	83.9
Bancroft	832	1,170	14.53	965	91
Cushing	105	1,754	23.48	301	18.4
Wiborg	138	1,303	19.96	373	25.6

WHY NOT CYCLE ABROAD YOURSELF?

L'AMERICAINE

BY CLARENCE STETSON

DOWN THE SIMPLON

LA PARISIENNE

www.ingramcontent.com/pod-product-compliance
Lightning Source LLC
Chambersburg PA
CBHW020900230426

43666CB00008B/1252